Haynes

Build your own
Gaming PC

© Haynes Publishing 2019

Adam Barnes has asserted his moral right to be identified as the author of this work.

First published November 2015
Reprinted October 2016 and February 2018
Revised and updated November 2019

Published by: Haynes Publishing
Sparkford, Yeovil, Somerset BA22 7JJ, UK
Tel: 01963 440635
Int. tel: +44 1963 440635
Website: www.haynes.com

British Library Cataloguing in Publication Data:
A catalogue record for this book is available from the British Library

ISBN 978 1 78521 668 8

Library of Congress control no. 2019942920

Printed in Malaysia

Haynes

Build your own Gaming PC

Adam Barnes

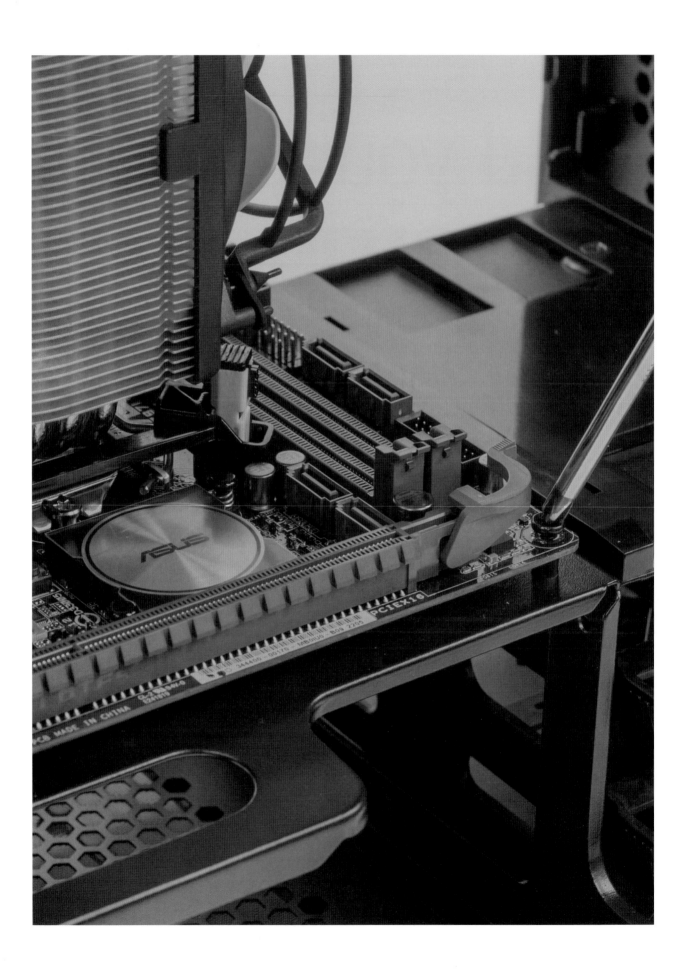

Contents

1

PART

Why build your own gaming PC?

With so many amazing options available to buy ready-made gaming PCs from brilliant makers like Chillblast.com and Overclockers.co.uk you may wonder why anyone would want to build their own gaming PC at all. After all, there's bound to be a system that suits your needs among the hundreds available, and that shiny new PC could be on your doorstep within 48 hours.

The answers are simple: choice, budget and upgradability. You have the opportunity to create an entirely custom PC designed specifically with your needs in mind and, regardless of what the marketing men would have you believe, you're the only one that can deliver it.

As you might already know, high-end gaming hardware tends to be more expensive than the average run-of-the-mill kit, so (like it or not) your available budget is going to play a very key role in the end result. But that's perhaps the biggest advantage of doing everything yourself; you're in control of absolutely everything and can dictate precisely where the money should go. Do you want a quick computer? The very best graphics from the top-end games? Or are you looking to multitask whenever you're on the machine? Answer questions like these and you'll find not only your needs, but the right budget to go with it.

PART **1**

Advantages of PC gaming

Perhaps the prevailing thought surrounding building a gaming PC is just how prohibitively expensive it is, but that's only true if you're not smart about your purchasing decisions. Sure, it'd be a simple task to pick out the most expensive parts and fit them all together, but while that could lead to issues of its own – compatibility being the biggest disaster you may encounter – it's also a fruitless endeavour in terms of power and gains. Building a gaming PC is about picking the right parts, and rule numero uno here comes first down to budget: knowing what you can afford and trying to stick to it rigidly will make the decision-making process considerably less daunting.

It might be scary to look at, but with the necessary information you'll find you have no problem installing any part of a PC; it's actually pretty simple these days.

Gaming PCs can come in all sorts of shapes and sizes, so it's not really as simple as picking one from a shelf. Knowing what you want is the first step.

And therein lies the first main advantage of PC gaming: its flexibility. Every PC owner is different and every gamer has their own tastes and wants. What those are will effectively control the requirements of your system, but because of this flexibility you can put together something that fulfils those needs as well as your budget. If you need a computationally powerful machine for faster processing, then that's where you need to spend the money. If high-end graphics are what you're hoping to achieve, then the GPU is the focus. Since the parts are chosen by you, there's no concern that the machine you have won't be in some way inferior to your particular needs. And in truth, buying an off-the-shelf gaming PC just won't have that guarantee of efficiency in conjunction with value for money.

On top of that, there's a sense that a gaming PC can also be a future project, too. If you don't have the funds to kit it out with the high-end gear you are dreaming of just yet, you can save on certain parts to build a functional and acceptable machine with the prospects of upgrading at a later date. And since you know the parts inside your computer, you'll more easily be able to figure out how and what can be swapped out for better equipment when the time comes to do so.

But the thing to know is that simply by choosing to self-build, you'll automatically be saving money. Whether you're buying a prebuilt gaming PC online or (shock horror!) in a physical store, there's always an added cost that comes with that. Yes, there's more manual effort involved this way, but that ultimately means you'll reduce the initial outlay. The fact that you're free to shop around for the cheapest price and buy when you find it at a price you're willing to pay only adds to the potential for savings.

PART ① Understanding your needs

When it comes to building a gaming PC you first need to ask yourself what it is you want to get out of the machine. High-end PC games can require a great deal of computing power to run at their very best, but that doesn't mean you need to spend over the odds for an enjoyable gaming experience. As already mentioned, your budget will play a major part in the sort of PC you can build, but you should also think about the types of games you're interested in playing, whether you'll be attending gaming competitions or even where you'll be keeping it – you don't want an ugly PC case if it's to sit opposite your living room TV, after all. With this in mind, we've identified three typical archetypes of gamers that additionally fit into three distinct price ranges.

Indie games are typified by their simpler, often 2D graphics, but that doesn't mean that they are any less interesting than the 'hardcore' releases.

The Indie Gamer

These days PC gaming isn't solely about bleeding-edge graphics. Over the past few years there's been a boom in what's known as 'indie gaming', which is to say games developed by small teams often no bigger than ten people. Naturally with the limited budgets of these developers, indie games are more constrained technically but typically produce much more innovative or experimental gameplay concepts that big budget developers just don't have the freedom to create.

And since the technical demands of these games are rarely intense (most indie games use 2D visuals rather than the more computing-intensive 3D graphics), the specs of a PC dedicated to these cool titles needn't be too demanding either. As a result, the cost of such a PC is far more budget-friendly and flexible, and while you could spend way over £1,000 there's no reason why you couldn't spend as little as £600 for a gaming PC that'll still last you a good few years.

But what's more, you'll still be able to play some high-end games in this category, too, though you'll need a savvy use of each game's graphical settings menu to get many of them to work smoothly. The beauty of a custom build means that you can spend more on elements like the graphics card if you do want to dabble in high-end 3D gaming, but ultimately you'll be looking at a system that'll age much quicker than our other example builds here. Take a look at our example of a low-end PC built with indie gaming in mind:

- Cooler Master K350 Mid-Tower Case
- Asus H81M-Plus Intel H81 Chipset Motherboard
- Intel Pentium G3240 3.1GHz Dual Core CPU
- EVGA GTX 750 Ti 2GB GPU
- Corsair Vengeance 1,600MHz 8GB RAM
- Seagate 7,200rpm 1TB HDD
- Corsair VS550 PSU

Since the budgets of indie game developers are significantly smaller, there are greater opportunities for innovation and invention. This is why they've become so popular as a sub-genre.

Esports are becoming increasingly popular both at a competitive level and as entertainment for viewers. This is largely why high-skill games like *Dota 2* or *League Of Legends* are so popular on Twitch.

Fortnite is one of the most played games, and consistently one of the most streamed (and watched). The bubble doesn't look set to burst just yet, either.

The Streamer

Streaming gameplay onto Twitch or recording videos for YouTube is an incredibly popular way of gaming, some driven by the huge success of big-name video content creators while others just enjoy having people to interact with and learn from while they're gaming. Since the big question first and foremost comes down to the sorts of games you'll want to stream, this will dictate the kind of hardware you'll need. It's worth remembering that, since the intention is to share your gameplay with the world, there's

a certain expectation of visual quality that people will expect; if they can't make out the game, why would they stay and watch?

With that said, you can still build a fairly capable machine around the £1,300 mark, which will allow for most games to be played at their near-best. You will likely want to grab accessories like a second monitor – which doesn't need to be as high resolution as your primary screen – or a decent microphone and webcam, but these come down to personal preference and how seriously you want to take your streaming sessions.

However, there are still some concessions you'll need to consider. Multitasking will be important, especially if you want a dual-monitor setup, so a multi-core processor is essential as is a larger amount of RAM. The games you'll play will dictate the graphics card you'll need and therefore the final price, so take a look at the recommended system requirements of the games that you fancy and get something similar or greater. Here's our recommendation for a mid-range PC designed for streaming:

- Bitfenix Prodigy Case
- Asus Z97I-Plus Motherboard
- Intel Core i5 4690K
- Arctic Cooling Freezer 7 Pro Rev 2 CPU cooler
- NVIDIA GeForce GTX 960 2GB
- Corsair 2000MHz DDR4 8GB RAM
- 1TB Seagate SSHD Hybrid drive
- Corsair CX600 PSU

The Pro Gamer

The definition of a 'pro gamer' is a fairly loose one and while it increasingly refers primarily to professional gamers – i.e. those competing at a high level at esports tournaments – it can also mean those level of gamers that are dedicated to the medium as a serious hobby. In either case, the demands of such a gamer is for a gaming PC that provides smooth gameplay for the highest-end games played at their visual best. What this means is a machine that can pump out any game at its 'Ultra' settings at a smooth 60FPS (or greater), ideally without much in the way of tweaking settings or being picky about the hardware.

As you might expect, this means spending quite a bit on some of the best parts available to gamers. Typically a pro gamer's PC will have a little more aesthetic flair to the case itself, various customisable LED lights, flashy fans or a case that is designed as much for its attractive looks as its raft of options for hardware. Of course, this all comes down to personal taste, but either way you'll be spending a good chunk of cash on a PC that fulfils the needs of a pro gamer.

But make no mistake, our suggested build here is by no means the top echelon of gaming PCs. In terms of horsepower it'll still offers no-holds-barred, high-end gaming with a full range of extras like solid-state storage drives, water cooling and the capacity for Scalable Link Interface (SLI) graphics cards. That's not the case here, but if you want the absolute best then aiming around a price range of £1,800–£2,000 will get you a gaming computer that'll see you right for years to come. Here's an example of a high-end gaming PC build:

- NZXT Source 340 Mid-Tower Case
- Gigabyte X99 Gaming 5 Motherboard
- Intel Haswell-E 5820K 3.30GHz CPU
- Corsair H100i water cooler
- MSI GeForce GTX 970 4GB
- G.Skill 2400MHz DDR4 16GB RAM
- Samsung 840 EVO 2.5in 250GB SSD
- Seagate 2TB SSHD 3.5in Hard Drive
- Corsair CX750 PSU

The term pro gamer is often synonymous with 'hardcore gamer', essentially denoting someone who plays all the latest and greatest games, from blockbuster shooters to the most intriguing indie games.

PART

What type of gamer are you?

So now you know, roughly speaking, the sort of PC you might want to build. But to really help guide yourself down the right path, you'll need to consider the type of gamer you are. While console games typically end up on PC, there are those that are specifically designed solely for computers and in that sense knowing which games you'll want to play will ultimately tell you what you're looking for. Here's a handy cheat sheet for figuring out the type of gamer you are.

MMOs like *World Of Warcraft* are typically exclusive to the PC platform, often because their depth, technical requirements and number of possible actions at any one time really benefit from the advantages a computer has over a console.

Strategy games are often better suited to PC due to the fact that they usually come with a lot of menus and buttons to click, so if you like games that get you thinking then PC gaming is for you.

FPS	Standing for first-person shooter, these games typically require high-end graphics and silky-smooth frame rates to be played at their best, especially if they're played online. PC gamers will swear that this platform is the only way to play an FPS, not only for the clear visual fidelity but also the advantage and greater skill that comes from the keyboard and mouse combo. Of all the genres prevalent on PC, it's perhaps the one that results in the largest number of pro gamers.	• You'll need a high-end graphics card to ensure the quality of visuals necessary for this genre. • Single-player FPS games are often some of the most intensive PC games around, so if this is your preference then you'll want a PC that can manage this. • When it comes to accessories, a monitor with a high refresh rate is important, as is a gaming mouse with a high DPI for fast-paced reactions.
MMO	Massively multiplayer online games have been popular for decades now, typified by huge worlds to explore, large numbers of players to interact with and a great variety to the experiences. Whether it's in space hunting for fortune or in a fantastical setting fighting wars against other factions, MMOs only really take place on PC.	• Since MMOs aren't typically graphically intensive, the focus here would be the CPU since it'll allow for the large number of objects and players to be loaded in quickly. • Storage options should be something to consider, too, since MMOs take up a lot of space. However, utilising an SSD will help load in the huge worlds much quicker. • The layout of your keyboard is important, too, since you'll usually want to hotkey a large number of skills as shortcuts.
MOBA	Almost exclusive to PC gaming, the MOBA is a hugely popular genre of game dominated largely by *League Of Legends*. This genre can vary between objectives and styles, but the most common is a 5v5 battle arena where player champions level up during a single multiplayer match in a bid to get an advantage over the opposing team.	• MOBAs just aren't that challenging for a PC since they're almost always played from a top-down perspective. Favouring speed with high amounts of memory and a snappy processor will get each match loading quickly. • A stable internet connection is also a boon, so if you can't connect via Ethernet then be sure to pick a Wi-Fi adapter that'll provide stable, high-speed transfers. • A high DPI gaming mouse is useful here, but one with additional buttons is a priority.
Open World	While open world games aren't exactly exclusive to PC, the advantage they have is that these games are empowered by systems that can quickly stream in data. It's also a very popular genre for modders, a tangent of PC gaming that can open up whole new games and experiences that consoles just can't.	• As a genre, open world games perhaps offer the widest range of settings, allowing for a broad spectrum of system specs. The more powerful that every key component of the machine is, the more you'll notice the difference in this genre of game. • Open world games usually rely on streaming data into and out of the active memory, so RAM and CPU are your best options here.
Strategy	Due to the menu-heavy gameplay of strategy games, PC gaming is better suited to the genre due to the mouse input. These can encompass turn-based, board game-like experiences such as *Civilization*, intensely fast-paced real-time strategy, or the huge subgenre of simulation games. The latter often focuses around building cities, running businesses or managing trade.	• While strategy games won't ever beat out first-person titles for visual fidelity, they can sometimes be surprisingly intensive on a GPU, so something that can handle this is a must. • With that said, a lot of the technical demands will be affected by your preference. City-building games naturally benefit from better graphics, while turn-based strategy games will want computational power to more quickly deal with the AI enemy teams.
Battle Royale	As the only genre here that can be considered 'new', battle royales are typified as multiplayer experiences where a large group of players compete to become the last one standing. The idea is to scavenge the world for incrementally better but randomly located weapons and items, while the play space becomes increasingly smaller, therefore causing the tension to rise. This makes it a genre well-suited to streaming.	• Most will have heard the name *Fortnite* in some capacity, and it was this game with its accessible system specs and simplification of the core gameplay that popularised the genre. However, other contenders to its throne try to distinguish themselves with greater visual fidelity and so a focus on graphical power is essential. • One thing worth pointing out is just how new the genre is, so there's unknown potential for these sorts of games to evolve in ways we can't predict.

PART  What to consider

This is all well and good, but the list of components is vast and overwhelming. We're confident that you could just pick the parts on each of our builds and fit them all together with no issues, but that's not going to work for everyone. Needs differ and the flexibility of building a gaming PC yourself is why it's even worth considering a self-build over a premade system bought online. As such, here's the things you should think about when deciding what your needs are and what you'll need.

Know the specs

While we'll go into closer detail about what to look for when buying hardware in later chapters, it's important to know first what sorts of games you want to play and pick the parts that'll match those needs. Knowing that you need a 4GB graphics card, for example, will automatically narrow down the options available to you.

Futureproofing

As with any technology, there's no such thing as a truly futureproof computer, least of all a gaming PC. However, if you're eager to build a machine that will sustain your gaming at a fair comfortability for several years, then you'll naturally need to spend a bit more on the hardware now to ensure it'll go the distance. This doesn't mean the most expensive parts, just those that are going to keep you going and have good recommendations for overclocking (discussed in a later chapter).

Form factor

In the majority of situations, you'll want a case that has a lot of space inside to allow for air to more effectively pass through the computer and therefore allow for better cooling. However, if portability or aesthetic appeal is important (perhaps the PC will be sitting in a very visible place), then consider a form factor to match; this means a motherboard to match and that ultimately necessitates which parts you can install, so this is a significant thing to think about.

Drives and ports

One of the most flexible aspects of any PC build is the drives that are installed. Do you really need a DVD drive? Would you rather have the quick boot-up time provided by an SSD? Or do you intend to fill your disk drive with gigabytes of data? Answers to these will affect what parts you'll need or want to include. Don't forget the ports, either, since these days you'll perhaps want to allow for USB Type-3 and Thunderbolt ports, particularly to allow for 4K monitors.

Connections

Outside of the ports, knowing how you're going to want to connect the PC to the world is important. In an ideal situation you'll want to just connect via Ethernet to the internet and so a Wi-Fi adapter is essentially useless; you'll almost always be downloading games, after all. And unless you're insistent on 7.1 surround sound, you can overlook extras like suitable connections for such needs. You don't need every extra that is advertised.

A beginner build

One last thing to ponder is whether you really need the top-end PC right now. Remember, by building it yourself you can choose parts that'll last well into the future and only upgrade certain parts as and when you need them. If you don't feel the need for 32GBs of memory right now – and arguably you won't – then go with your minimum need and add to it over time. The same can be true for all other parts: by buying cheaper, less impressive parts now you can splash the cash on a new upgrade in a couple of years as and when demand dictates.

PART  # The tools of the trade

Since most modern computer components snap together more like elaborate LEGO for grown-ups than precision electronic components, you really don't need to have anything particularly special to hand to help you build your gaming PC. That said, there are a handful of items and considerations to keep in mind.

Anti-static

There are a few hurdles and stumbling blocks to bear in mind. The first of these is any electronic device's nemesis: static electricity. Is it possible to kill a £450 graphics card simply by taking it out of its anti-static bag? Yes, absolutely, and it really can happen.

Before you handle any of your gaming PC's prized components you should ground yourself. The briefest touch of the nearest radiator or pipework will do the trick provided you're not then scuffing your feet back along nylon carpet to your workbench. Another solution is to use an anti-static wristband. It'll help stop the natural build-up of static electricity but is far from a requirement.

Cable ties

Something you'll hear quite a lot about as we guide you through the process of building your own PC in this book is airflow and the need to keep your computer as cool as possible. Heat is your enemy. It shortens the lives of your components and it makes for a noisier PC (more fans working harder to keep temperatures down). One of the easiest ways to help keep temperatures down inside your PC is to ensure that the flow of air through your case from the front, or top, to the rear 'exhaust' of your PC is free from the jumble of cables inside your case. The easiest way to tame this tangle is with some carefully placed cable ties. They're very cheap and disposable – you don't have to use them sparingly.

Phillips screwdriver

Last, but certainly not least, is the humble Phillips screwdriver. Believe it or not, this is the only tool you need (though it doesn't hurt to have a small pair of long-nosed pliers to hand). The beauty of most modern gaming cases is the fact that they offer almost completely tool-less construction. Almost everything can be slotted or clipped or screwed (and even then most screws are thumbscrews, meaning they can be done by hand).

Installing software

You may notice that we haven't included a DVD (optical) drive in any of our builds. That's largely because no one involved in the making of this book has touched a DVD or compact disc of any kind in the last five years. We appreciate that might not apply to everyone and some readers might wonder how they're supposed to install Windows or a Linux distribution like Ubuntu or Steam OS.

For Windows you simply need to download an official ISO (disk image) from Microsoft and their handy USB tool, which you can find at http://windows.microsoft.com/en-GB/windows-8/ create-reset-refresh-media. All you need is an 8GB USB stick.

Now that Steam OS, the Linux-based operating system powering Steam Machines, has over 1,000 supported games you might want to give that a try. For full instructions for installing it via a USB stick just visit http://store.steampowered.com/steamos.

2

PART  # Anatomy of a gaming PC

On the face of it, building your own gaming PC sounds like a difficult and complicated task that could turn into an engineering marathon. While it is certainly true that you could spend months building a modified case with a custom liquid-cooling system, it is also possible to slap the hardware together in less than an hour.

Perhaps that sounds impossible, but think about it in the sum of its parts. With the case open, it's just a matter of installing the power supply and the motherboard then adding in the CPU, memory, graphics card and any storage or media drives on top of that. Perhaps this sounds a little dismissive of what might seem like a complicated job to a newcomer, but in truth modern computer hardware has been standardised so much over the years that it's pretty much a case of plug and play. So long as you're methodical and follow your connections properly, the machine can be up and running with minimal fuss in less time than it takes to install Windows.

However, as with so many things, a lot of the success of the work is in the planning stage. If you plan the job poorly, you may spend some time shopping for a power supply extension cable or a cooling fan that is essential to finish the job. We should also sound a note of caution: if you order incompatible parts (such as the wrong memory or processor), you may find yourself in the position where it is impossible to complete your PC build without ordering a replacement component.

PART 2 Understanding the basics

Let's start at the beginning with a list of components. If you dismantle pretty much any PC you will end up with a motherboard, processor, memory, graphics, cooling, SSD/hard drive, case and power supply. While it is also common to find a DVD or Blu-Ray drive, this is not strictly necessary and these days networking and audio are likely to be features that are integrated as part of the motherboard where once they would have been separate expansion cards.

The core of any computer is the motherboard, which houses and connects all of the hardware together.

You will often hear a particular component called by different names, so a mainboard is the same thing as a motherboard, a graphics card is a VGA (Video Graphics Adapter), a case is an enclosure and RAM (Random Access Memory) is also called system memory.

There is no escaping the fact that the computer industry loves acronyms. In addition to VGA and RAM, you will doubtless come across CPU (Central Processing Unit), PSU (Power Supply Unit), HDD (Hard Disk Drive), SSD (Solid State Drive) and many more. You do not necessarily need to understand what each and every acronym means, but once in a while you need to stop and double-check the alphabet soup isn't leading you astray. It is all too easy to look at a graphics card with DVI-I and HDMI outputs (they are different types of connections for displays and TVs) and note that your intended 4K display also has HDMI to lead you to think: 'Yes, that works, I just need an HDMI cable.' But following that train of thought can lead you down a faulty path; technically speaking the connection will work, but is it the best option for your system?

That's why it's so crucial to understand not only what your needs are, but what each of the parts do. We will be covering the specifics of each piece of hardware in closer detail later in this chapter, but it's still important to know the basics of how it all connects together and works. Initially it could well be overwhelming with the sheer amount of confusing technical details you'll encounter, but take it a step at a time. First it's important to just get a sense for some general numbers and, through that, an understanding of the system you'll need to build. To be reductionist about it, and to help you overcome that initial first hurdle, we've selected what is widely considered to be the three most crucial parts to running a video game:

	CPU	GPU	RAM
Purpose:	The Central Processing Unit, or simply processor, is commonly referred to as the 'brain' of any computer. It's the part that doles out and controls every process of the machine, allotting computational power to their respective hardware as and when their demands increase or decrease. Within a game, it's the CPU that is dedicated to logical calculations, meaning the AI of characters not controlled by the player, physics systems and anything that requires loading in data quickly.	As the name might suggest, the Graphics Processing Unit has the duty of producing the visuals for your games. While there is a misconception that it is exclusively dedicated to 3D graphics, this is only partially correct in that 2D games simply don't challenge a GPU in the same way. It is designed to handle one specific job, pushing pixels and rendering shapes. Unlike the CPU, which is more of a multitasker, a GPU is specialised in its purpose. If high-end graphics are your goal, then a high-end GPU will ultimately be the means to this end.	The system memory or Random Access Memory is the piece of hardware that essentially controls how quickly your computer can think. It's a cache of sorts, with data and processes loaded into its storage from the moment your computer is switched on to the moment it's shut down. Active processes – and by that we might software being used or actions being undertaken in the background – all feed off the RAM. The CPU chooses what is loaded into the memory, but once it's been loaded in the same process takes less time to complete. More RAM means better multitasking, quicker load times and more software active at once.
What to look for:	The big number that is advertised with CPUs is its speed, measured in GHz. The bigger this is, the faster the processor can 'think'. However, it's also important to have a CPU that can multitask, so picking one with multiple cores (four is a minimum these days) is essential.	In truth, there are far more crucial things to know about a GPU purchase than any of the three here. With that said, the sheer amount of data it can process is usually the focus when it comes to system specifications. In this sense, looking for the number of gigabytes (GB) of memory on board the GPU is your starting point.	There are certain factors here that go beyond sheer numbers, especially when it comes to compatibility, but luckily with RAM it can often be as simple as picking the biggest number. This is measured gigabytes, though knowing how many individual sticks of memory you're getting is important since your motherboard will have limited space.

Now, any gaming machine is the sum of its parts. If there is a bottleneck in one area, then it doesn't matter how highly specced the rest of the computer is, it's going to have issues overcoming that restriction. Having less system memory, for example, will ultimately limit how much you can have running on the machine before it begins to stutter, slow down or even crash. Don't worry, this isn't likely to happen with a sensibly considered gaming PC, but it's certainly worth knowing that your build needs to be researched properly to ensure you'll have what it takes to run the games you want to play.

With that in mind, there is a handy means of figuring that out that doesn't require too much in the way of technical knowledge of each piece of hardware. Minimum and recommended system requirements can be very useful in creating an initial guideline; these are the hardware expectations that the developers of the games themselves believe are necessary to enjoy the game at an acceptable level. Once upon a time you'd find these in a corner on the back of the DVD case, but since almost all PC games are delivered digitally these days, instead you'll need to look either at the details within the digital store or simply search for the game's name alongside 'system requirements'.

Remember, though, that while this can be a good guideline for what you need, it isn't necessarily what you want. Even the recommended specs are by no means the tippity top of the possible scale. In fact, with so many graphics settings available to customise the visuals and many PC games designed to run on as broad a range of computers as possible (not to mention the inferior hardware found in games consoles), the recommended system requirements needs to be taken as a guideline and not a strict rule. Computer hardware can move at an incredible pace, so targeting today's recommended specs will likely leave you with a machine that will age much sooner than one that has been properly built with a lasting appeal.

With the knowledge that recommended specs should be a jumping-off point rather than a shopping list, let's take a look at some of the guidelines for the different sorts of games you could be playing:

FPS

Game:	*Overwatch*	*Battlefield 1*
Recommended system specs:	CPU: Intel Core i5 or AMD Phenom II X3 GPU: Nvidia GeForce GTX 660 or ATI Radeon HD 7950 RAM: 6GB	CPU: Intel Core i7 4790K or AMD Ryzen 3 1300X GPU: Nvidia GeForce GTX 1060 6GB or AMD Radeon RX 480 8GB RAM: 12GB

The newest technology taking over gaming is real-time ray tracing, which simulates realistic environmental lighting.

While *Overwatch* isn't the freshest game available, regular releases of new content and thriving esports and content streaming scenes have maintained its status as one of the most popular FPS games. It's a good study subject for researching, though, since its cartoony visuals can still be rather demanding, though the recommended GPU won't pump out the highest resolutions. *Battlefield 1*, on the other hand, favours realism and high-end visual effects thanks to the special Frostbite engine that is powering it. The requirements of the latter are significantly greater, though it's interesting to note that the minimum GPU of *Battlefield 1* is the same as the recommended one for *Overwatch*.

Ultimately, *Battlefield 1* is a very good test for what you might want to aim for if first-person gaming is your thing. Each of the recommended parts here are at the top of the scale and will keep your system going for quite some years. The *Battlefield* games are well known for showcasing the latest technologies of video game graphics, so it's not a bad benchmark to aim for.

Strategy

Game:	Planet Coaster	Total War: Three Kingdoms
Recommended system specs:	CPU: Intel Core i7-4770 3.90 GHz or AMD FX-8350 4.0GHz GPU: Nvidia GeForce GTX 980 4GB or AMD R9 380 4GB RAM: 12GB	CPU: Intel Core i5 6600 or AMD Ryzen 5 2600X GPU: Nvidia GeForce GTX 970 or AMD R9 Fury X 4GB RAM: 8GB

Despite being a few years old now, *Planet Coaster* is still a great example of just how intensive the simulation branch of strategy games can be. Admittedly, newer comparable games might offer more contemporary insight for potential builders, for instance *Anno 1800* has far heftier requirements and certainly has the advanced visuals to go with it. But *Planet Coaster* is the premier example of a modern simulation game, and highlights just how complex a game's systems could be: high-end visuals, physics calculations of the roller coasters, AI computation of your park's guests – *Planet Coaster* has it all, and it shows in its specs. *Total War*, on the other hand, is a whole different story. These are games about managing large armies in graphically impressive, realistic battles. Interestingly it, too, has real-time AI calculations, high-end visuals and physics-based computation with ammunition. Despite this, it doesn't recommend the absolute pinnacle of gaming hardware to play well, so it's a good estimation of what to aim for if strategy gaming might be your thing.

Planet Coaster might not feel like an intensive game because of its cartoony visuals, but there's actually a complex AI system controlling the crowd.

Battle Royale

Game:	*Fortnite*	*Apex Legends*
Recommended system specs:	CPU: Intel Core i5 2.8 GHz GPU: Nvidia GeForce GTX 660 2GB or AMD Radeon HD 7870 2GB RAM: 8GB	CPU: Intel Core i5 3570K 3.4GHz GPU: Nvidia GeForce GTX 970 4GB or AMD Radeon RX 290 4GB RAM: 8GB

The battle royale genre has grown in popularity rapidly over the last few years, and so it could evolve in any number of ways from here.

Though the battle royale genre is spawning a new entry with every day, currently the ones to beat are *Fortnite* from Epic Games and *Apex Legends* from Respawn Entertainment. They each go down distinctly different routes, with *Fortnite* favouring exaggerated, cartoony visuals while *Apex Legends* is a little more serious if not in tone then at least in look. They're both large, open world multiplayer gaming experiences, however, so there's little wiggle room in terms of technical requirements.

As you'll see, though, the emphasis on accessibility has meant that *Fortnite* demands less from its players than *Apex Legends*, but don't fall into the trap of thinking that 'cartoony' graphics equates less computational power; there are plenty of post-processing effects that require certain games to match Pixar-like visual quality, so remember it's always important to check the system requirements. Note, also, that both games require more in the GPU department than the CPU or RAM – a side effect of the genre, which doesn't have much in the way of computational gameplay.

PART  Research your build

It is pretty much impossible to pluck a price for a gaming PC from the air as there is such a huge variety of hardware. You can, however, say that £799 is a good starting point (for the tower, minus the monitor, mouse and keyboard), £999 is a psychological landmark, £1,299 gets you plenty and £1,999 is 'Ulp, how much?' If you go for the absolute maximum it is possible to spend £4,000, £6,000 or £8,000 on a gaming PC. To put that in context, some of us take a week's holiday in Cornwall or Spain while others head to the West Indies or safari in Kenya.

The easiest way to start drafting the specification of your new gaming PC is to look at the website of one of the smaller PC builders. They will doubtless offer an array of PCs that you can customise using a series of drop-down menu options to select the components. While it won't help with understanding precisely what you need, it will rapidly give you a clear idea about the current state of gaming hardware and the cost of the components.

Let's break down a £1,200 PC build to get an idea of where the money goes and give you a sort of checklist for parts you need to add on your own list. There is a range of prices for each component, but broadly speaking we can say:

£400 on a 6GB graphics card
£150 on an Intel i5 CPU
£100–£150 on the motherboard
£80 on the case
£70 for a copy of Windows 10
£60–£70 for 16GB of DDR4 memory
£60 on a 500GB solid-state drive
£50–£70 on a 2TB or 3TB hard drive
£50–£60 on the power supply
£40 for air cooler for your CPU
£20 for a DVD drive
Total – circa £1,200

These prices are just guidelines to illustrate how you might break down the cost of a decent gaming PC, but in practice you can spend less on every component, or you can spend much more. The point here is to illustrate which components eat the bulk of the money, which is why the components are listed roughly in order of cost.

One thing is for certain: if you take a £799, £999, £1,299 or £1,999 PC from any of the manufacturers and break it down, you won't be able to build the same PC yourself for the same price. The fact you are paying retail prices means it will cost you more to build exactly the same PC and that's without allowing for the time you will invest or the convenience of having an assembled PC delivered to your door complete with a warranty.

That might make these prebuilt machines seem tempting, but that's overlooking the whole point of building your own system: flexibility. Sure these machines are going to get you up and running quicker and easier and for a comparative price, but you won't ever have exactly the PC you want, and if you shop around smartly you'll find yourself able to find alternatives to the parts in these prebuilt rigs that are just as good and perhaps cheaper.

Of course, the starting point to this comes down to knowledge; knowing what to look for with each part will give you the tools you need to make that final purchasing decision. Your needs and wants plays into this, and combined with an understanding of what each part is for and what technical details you need to pay attention to will help you to follow the checklist of necessary hardware and pick out the specific purchases one by one. You might have a different way of doing things, but methodically going through a list and finding potential options will make it seem like a much less overwhelming process. We're going to cover each part in greater detail following on from this and in an order that will help with compatibility.

You could buy a custom-built PC from a number of online retailers, even going so far as to pick the parts you want, but you still won't have full control.

PART  Motherboards

There's no other way of looking at it: graphics cards are easily one of the most important parts of any gaming PC. They will be doing the brunt of the graphical work after all. But that's not where you should start, and nor is it the processor. Almost everything built into your PC will be added onto the motherboard, and so it's crucial to start here first and foremost. Knowing roughly what sort of level of machine you're building will ultimately guide the decision on a motherboard level, because knowing you'll want a water-cooled system with two GPUs and a huge stack of memory will let you know just how much space you'll need. Knowing your needs will help you nail down the form factor, which is a little like deciding whether your ideal accommodation would be an apartment, bungalow, house or mansion. The form factor has a huge impact on the finished gaming PC, and the main consideration boils down to the parts you'll hope to include.

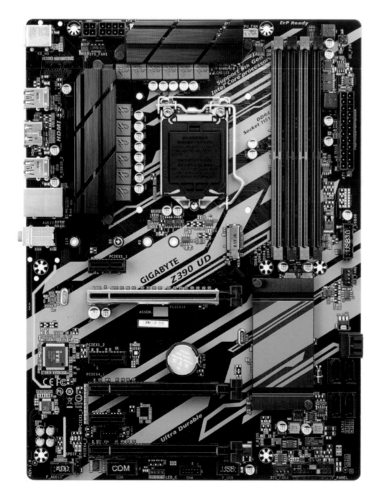

Ultimately the decision comes down to the available slots on the motherboard itself. We'll explain the exact terminology shortly, but think of the motherboard like one of those toys kids play with that requires them to fit certain shapes into specific holes. It's much the same here: memory will fit into the memory slots, GPUs will fit into the GPUs slots, the processor sits in the sole position for the CPU. That's a gross generalisation, of course, but this is all to say that knowing what you'll have to fit into the machine will ultimately dictate the form factor or your motherboard. Will you have four RAM modules? Then you'll need to have four slots for it to fit into.

There are two key considerations, then, the chipset – which equates almost directly to the number of parts that can be installed – and the form factor, essentially the shape, size and general layout of the motherboard. The hard part is picking a manufacturer of the board, and that's not an easy job any way you slice it. Gigabyte, Asus, MSI and ASRock are some of the big names in motherboards and so choosing popular products from any of these will make for safer choices but as with any kind

Motherboards can be the most intimidating parts, not only for the sheer number of compatibilities and potential options that are available, but they also look quite technical, too.

of technology purchase, you should try to find user and professional reviews to give you a bit of confidence that your pick is perfect.

Form factor

There are something like 40 different form factors that have been sorted out by the computer industry to ensure that a given motherboard will fit inside a particular case and work with a certain power supply, but happily we can safely ignore any obsolete, obscure or irrelevant form factors since a gaming machine is far more standard than a PC built for large-scale data storage, for instance.

For gaming PCs, the mainstream form factor is ATX and will offer the most expansion slots – meaning spaces to install hardware like the graphics card. With this space it gives the manufacturer plenty of scope to design their motherboard to offer a fair amount of variety. A bigger board doesn't mean you should fill it all, however, since the more space there is between hardware the better air can circulate inside the case and therefore avoid overheating. ATX is the standard for a reason but, of all the options available, it provides the most flexibility for installable parts while still allowing for decent cable management and air circulation.

Some retailers sell motherboard sets with the RAM, processor and sometimes even a dedicated CPU cooler already installed.

The size of your PC case will control the size of your motherboard. A smaller Mini ITX has more restrictions, of course, but it's still possible to build a tiny powerhouse.

Outside of this there is the Micro ATX and Mini ITX, both of which are smaller. The Micro ATX is a good middle ground between less space but still offering a decent number of expansion slots. These are still good alternatives to the ATX and don't necessarily come with much compromise. The Mini ITX, on the other hand, is the smallest of the three and naturally is more restrictive about what you can install, but so long as you're not aiming for the highest end of gaming tech then it could be an option for those looking to build a PC that won't take up too much space and is incredibly more portable. It's worth adding that there are also the larger extremes of the E-ATX or XL-ATX, but if you're considering a system that requires this amount of space then you're already intending on a machine that is way beyond these initial, tentative steps into PC building.

Chipset

This is where the alphabet soup is at risk of confusing because you'll need to make sure that the chipset on your processor matches that of your motherboard. They simply won't work otherwise. It's manufacturer specific, too, so if you choose an Intel CPU then you need a motherboard that corresponds. Frustratingly, the chipset you use does matter, and to make matters worse it's an area that is updated on a regular basis. The core reason to focus on this is because the speed data transfer that a chipset is capable of ultimately affects how little bottlenecking there is between the processor and the processes of your system, and that includes the compatible speeds of your RAM.

On the Intel side you have the enthusiast Z370 and Z390, while the H370 and B360 are more general chipsets suitable for gamers. AMD is a little fairer with its longevity, and currently the Ryzen AM4 socket range of processors should last for some time. In that sense, chipsets X370 and X470 are on the enthusiast side, while a wider range of budget options means there are a greater range for gamers to choose from and won't necessarily limit the options for future enhancements.

Both Intel and AMD offer very high-end chipsets – X299 versus X399 respectively – for equally high-end processors, but these are certainly on the extreme end of the scale. It's not that they aren't going to give you the very best in gaming power, but in truth the technical boost here is hardly worth the exorbitant prices that these come with.

Expansion slots

To generalise somewhat, the expansion slot is the specific spaces created by the manufacturer of any given motherboard. There are a specific number of connections that are available with any high-level design of a motherboard (which is largely set by either Intel or AMD for that specific chipset). However, how those individual connections are divvied up is entirely down to the manufacturer: one board might have three PCIe 3.0 x16 slots, three PCIe 3.0 x1 slots and 1 M.2 slot, while another could have two PCIe 3.0 x16 slots, four PCIe 3.0 x1 slots and two M.2 slots. The number and type of expansion slots available will control the absolutely maximum configuration of installable parts, so if you want to run a dual-GPU setup then you'll need to make sure you've got two PCIe 3.0 x16 slots available.

It's worth understanding that PCIe – meaning PCI Express – is the standard for expansion cards these days, with the number that follows (x1, x4, x8 or x16) referring to the size of each slot. This is how you can know what will fit where: a GPU will take up a x16 slot and won't fit into a smaller PCIe x4 slot that is commonly used for cards like Wi-Fi adapters. However, even PCIe comes with its own versions within the category, and while it's not likely to be such a crucial thing to consider, the evolving nature of computer hardware does mean that you should always double-check that the expansion cards you buy will actually function with your motherboard's available expansion slots.

We also mentioned there the M.2 slot, a connection type that is common in laptops but has become increasingly more popular in PC hardware thanks to the small form factor of these drives – most regularly used for solid-state drives. We'll get on to that when we discuss storage options, but most modern motherboards will come with at least one slot.

Picking a good quality manufacturer is the hardest challenge if you have no prior knowledge, but online reviews will help pick the wheat from the chaff.

Memory

On top of expansion slots, you'll need to also take a look at the maximum memory capacity. This is typically presented with two sets of numbers, first the absolute maximum – say 64GB – and then a figure that explains how many individual memory bays there are. For instance, if a motherboard supports 4x16GB, then that means there are four individual memory bays, each with a maximum capacity of 16GB – giving you a figure that you can know is the absolute limit for your system.

It's also important to consider the potential speed available to you. Some motherboards – or rather, some chipsets – are limited to only DDR3 memory, which are slower than the increasingly standard DDR4. Even within those categories you may find the speed of the memory to be a restriction. If a chipset will only allow for memory speeds of up to 2,666MHz, then there's no sense in doling out extra for high-end 3,200MHz memory. Much like a supercar sitting in traffic in the centre of town, that memory can achieve much faster but it's being held in check and is essentially wasted money spent on potential it can't ever achieve.

Input/Output

Perhaps the area that is given the least amount of attention, the input/output (or I/O for short) specs of a motherboard details the types of connections that can be natively made with a motherboard. This essentially means that anything that can be plugged into the back of the computer that has a direct interaction with the motherboard. Once upon a time these were far more limited, but these days standardisation has allowed for a lot of the core requirements to be included: display and audio output, internet cable input, and connections for keyboards and mice are all made available as part of a motherboard.

But that doesn't mean there aren't things to pay attention to. On-board Wi-Fi or Bluetooth might be crucial for some, and they aren't common on gaming motherboards unless you pay a little extra for it. If it's a necessity for you – and it may well be – then either opt for a motherboard with these features on board, or buy a Wi-Fi adapter to do the work for you.

Elsewhere, connections like the USB 3.1 or Thunderbolt 3 will be useful at some point if not right away, while audiophiles might want to consider spending more to ensure the quality of a motherboard's audio output capabilities. However, in these cases you're probably better with a dedicated sound card to produce 5.1 or greater surround sound. Ultimately, think about your immediate needs and the connections that

might come with them, and then confirm that your would-be motherboard will allow for these.

Overclocking or Dual-GPU?

We have a section dedicated to overclocking later in the manual, but for now we'll say this: overclocking isn't something that an amateur PC builder is going to want to busy themselves with at first. Despite that, both this and dual-GPU setups are something you do need to consider from the start of the build. Not all motherboards allow for these functions, so if you think it might be something you'd like to consider, then you'll have to make greater efforts to look for boards that are designated as ready for this. When it comes to dual-GPU setups, you'll need to look for either SLI-ready or CrossFire-ready motherboards. These types of builds are far more technical and require much more consideration, and often dual-GPUs aren't actually more effective than a single GPU with equal power. It's a specialist thing, really; something to think about for a future build, perhaps.

The important thing to remember when buying a motherboard is to pair it with the right chipset of your processor.

PART  Central Processing Unit (CPU)

Let's talk about processors. Specifically, let's talk about the CPU (Central Processing Unit), as opposed to the GPU (Graphics Processing Unit) or even the APU (Accelerated Processing Unit). The CPU is often referred to as the brain of your computer, but silicon can't really think for itself. In fact, the CPU is just a very clever calculator that performs mathematical calculations measured in billions per second.

The problem with this analogy is that the CPU sends this torrent of numbers back and forth around the PC and in particular feeds a stream of data to your graphics card(s) where it is rendered as jaw-droppingly awesome pictures on your monitor(s). If you follow that way of thinking, the CPU is more like the heart of your PC than the brain, but no matter how you imagine it the CPU is hugely important.

The elaborate packaging is one thing, but the i9 9900K is one of the top-end, mainstream processors at the moment.

The first step is to select the family of CPU that you want to use. This will enable you to settle on a particular CPU socket and a narrow selection of motherboard chipsets, and when you combine that with your chosen form factor you will be in a better position to choose the motherboard for your new PC.

There are only two mainstream contenders for the CPU market: AMD who has been playing the mouse to Intel's rather intimidating cat.

There are a number of features you need to consider when you compare one CPU with another, and we're going to look at those individually in turn. It is undoubtedly one of the most important – and most expensive – purchases you'll make for your gaming PC, but it does come with its own set of acronyms and jargon. Everything from the socket to the number of cores will likely confuse the layman. So rather than throw some examples into the mix and leave it at that, we're first going to run down each of the elements you'll come across when buying a CPU.

Socket

What the term 'socket' denotes is simply the type of mechanical connection the processor chip has with the motherboard. Its purpose is to help you buy compatible parts and so long as you buy a motherboard that matches the socket type then, at least at a mechanical level, you'll have parts that fit together. Ordinarily you'll be looking at a socket 1151 for Intel CPUs and the AM4 for AMD chips, but these can change from one day to the next; so long as the sockets match up with your motherboard, there are few other reasons to worry about this element.

AMD's Ryzen range is Its current selection, cheaper than an Intel equivalent but a fair alternative all the same.

Cores

If we do consider a CPU to be a computer's brain, then the number of cores essentially denotes just how many brains it has. Back in the day a computer would have a single chip with which it could calculate computations, with the speed of that particular chip affecting how fast those processes would be. Nowadays CPUs can have multiple cores, giving them the ability to multi-task far more easily. This is especially important for video games, where computations in physics systems and light rendering need to be performed while data needs to be streamed to the graphics card and hard drive – the more cores you have the more capable your machine is. It's worth familiarising yourself with the sorts of games you're playing, though. Multi-core processors are so prevalent these days that games developers know they can pretty much guarantee that they'll have the multi-processing capabilities of at least four cores. However, it might be tempting to think more cores equals more power, and that's not quite true; unless a program, game or tool has been developed specifically to make use of more cores, there likely won't be any advantage in spending over the odds to increase the number and speed of those cores.

If you find you're likely to take part in processor-intensive activities, however, such as 3D design or video editing and rendering, then you may want to consider aiming for more cores rather than more speed. Quad core is the most common you'll come across, though cheaper CPUs can come with dual cores while six and eight cores are on the way to superseding the long-time standard four cores – even if their costs are still a little prohibitive at the moment. Ultimately it comes down to a choice: if you're going to be regularly putting strain on your computer with computation-heavy processes and regularly multi-tasking in these situations, then you'll want to get yourself a CPU with a larger number of cores. If gaming is all you're aiming for, then a quad-core chip will more than satisfy your needs.

Number of threads

In truth this is almost always correlative to the number of cores your CPU has. If there are four cores, it's highly likely there are four threads. Unless specifically told otherwise, processors will always complete the first task they're given before moving on to the next, and so the number of threads refers to the total number of applications able to be executed on the CPU at any one time. Four cores, four threads, four applications. However, some processors offer a feature known as simultaneous multi-threading – or hyperthreading for Intel processors – whereby the operating system is told there are in fact twice the number of logical cores. While this doesn't actually increase the number of cores available, it allows for the processor to multi-task two applications per core and switch tasks far more easily. It's not a key aspect in CPU buying, but it's a nice added extra to look out for.

Core size

Measured in nanometers (nm) and relative to a single core on the CPU, the core size measurement is a factor you can largely ignore. If you're building a fairly typical computer – regardless of your budget – you'll likely encounter the numbers 14nm, 22nm or 32nm when it comes to a CPU's core size. If you're getting into the minutiae of hardware purchasing then it's worth knowing that a smaller core size will result in more efficient power consumption and computation speed, and in this regard Intel chips are currently ahead of the curve. But in truth the core size is a fairly insignificant factor to take into account when compared to some of the far more integral stats; don't be afraid to overlook core size when hunting for processors.

Core name

This is little more than the terminology given by the manufacturer – basically Intel or AMD – for the particular make and model of the cores installed on the processor. These are changing all the time, and even within particular families of chips the particular core model is often upgraded, changed or improved. Take, for example, Intel's latest iSeries of processors, which began life named Sandy Bridge, became Ivy Bridge and have since moved onto the likes of Coffee Lake and Cascade Lake. The particular name of a model will forever be changing, and that's not something we can really help with; you can usually spot the most up-to-date and recent chipset via the price (newer models will cost more), but don't be afraid to search for the information if you're at a loss. The name itself is irrelevant, but it's an easy way to spot-check just how new the CPU you're buying is, providing you research the most recent chipset of the series.

Unfortunately with PC hardware you'll often encounter silly names like 'Threadripper', often having very little meaning beyond marketing spin.

Clock/Turbo speed

Most CPUs will come with two measurements with regards to their speed: 'Clock' and 'Turbo'. The term clock is something you'll come across a lot when tinkering with your PC, and essentially it refers to a measurement of speed when compared to the computer's internal, mechanical clock – by which everything on the system is timed. A CPU's clock speed, then, is its base speed, and is used to detail the speed at which the processor will run when it is not under load. This is an important stat, for sure, since the processor should never drop below this speed, but since you'll be gaming on this PC – and therefore tasking your processor – you should also take note of the turbo speed. This is how fast the processor can run when it is under load – or, in other words, being used to compute intensive tasks like gaming – and will essentially denote its maximum capacity. This is actually one of the most important elements to look out for on your hardware purchasing travels, and should be a factor you take seriously when buying parts.

FSB/QPI/UPI/DMI/HT speed

Are these acronyms really all that important? Well, yes and no. Each acronym refers to the type of 'bus' used in the processor. A computer's 'bus' – as you might expect from its name – is the vehicle through which data is transferred from the CPU to the rest of the hardware. The speed of this part, then, will affect the speed with which other elements – such as your graphics card or memory – can receive and send back data to the central brain of your computer. As with a bus that you might travel on, the faster it travels the quicker it arrives at its destination. The acronyms, however, aren't all that important in and of themselves. FSB is perhaps the most common, albeit increasingly outdated, while newer ones – such as DMI – can transfer up to 20 Gigatransfers a second (GT/s). You may also find this measured in MHz – or megahertz – and there is a distinction. MHz is a bus's speed, while GT/s is the number of transfers it can make. While speed is important when it comes to your computer's bus, modern architecture demands that the number of transfers capable of being made is equally important. In that regard a bus's width is often more important than its speed; to use the transportation analogy again, if a bus can carry twice as many people, at max capacity it is able to transport more passengers than a smaller yet slightly quicker bus. Thankfully you don't really need to worry too much about the methodology of it all; just understand that the higher this number is – however it is measured – the better for your system's overall performance.

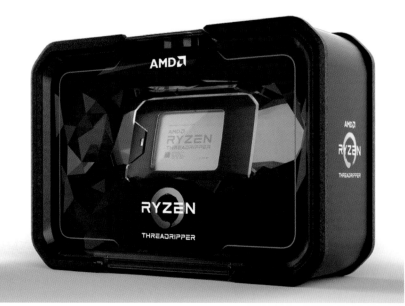

Voltage, wattage and temperature

The last thing you're going to want to look out for is the power consumption of your CPU, though in truth it's rare that this will ever impact (or even differ between) your purchasing decisions. As with all parts in your machine, the power that your CPU uses correlates to the temperature that it will run at – the more power, the higher the temperature. This is the single most important aspect of careful maintenance, because when your parts run too hot they are at a risk of becoming damaged. You may not get all of the information regarding these attributes, or you may only get its power consumption rather than the temperature (or vice versa), so try to use comparable parts as a reference point. It's most important to take note of the CPU's TDP (Thermal Design Power), which is the point at which the CPU is too hot to function. While this likely won't ever be a problem under ordinary circumstances, if it does overheat it will likely throttle the performance of the processor, making your machine run incredibly slowly or, in worst-case scenarios, shut off the CPU altogether. If you overclock your machine (which we'll talk about later), or find you are regularly stressing your CPU beyond its TDP, then you'll need to take precautions to ensure the problem is resolved – either by adding more cooling systems to your PC, reducing any overclocking you have done, or even replacing the thermal paste of the CPU.

Intel or AMD?

This is a common question when it comes to CPUs, but in truth the answer is rather easy to provide. While there are a handful of other CPU designers on the market, most are aimed at specialised markets – mobile, low-power consumption and the like – rather than more general-purpose hardware. When it comes to PC gaming, the processor industry really is a two-horse race, and the current leader has been ahead in the race for years.

Intel's control of the CPU market – as it stands – is unwavering. Its most recent iSeries range – i3, i5, i7 and i9 – has proven very popular, a fine balance between efficiency and power and a stability that all hardware purchasers hope for. It maintains its Pentium and Celeron range for low-budget alternatives – not something we really need to concern ourselves with – as well as its Xeon range, which offers many more cores per CPU than the typical quad core. This range is more in line with large-scale servers for businesses and – again – not really something we need

to consider. As such it's the iSeries that you'll want to look into for a gaming PC, and though the cost is slightly increased over an AMD equivalent, it's worth drawing attention to the company's reputation – there's no smoke without fire, as they say, and Intel is well known for producing high-quality processors that are well worth their cost.

AMD, on the other hand, has been struggling for years under the dominance of Intel. The difference is that Intel also manufactures its CPUs, so it is able to more easily implement new methods of production as it innovates on its designs. AMD's answer to this is to provide its CPUs at a cheaper price, hoping to clean up the budget market. As with Intel it manages lines for low-end and server-focused CPUs, with its current Ryzen range being the one for gamers. The difference here – besides price – is AMD's emphasis on extra cores, with an eight-core processor coming out at around the same price as a quad-core Intel equivalent. As discussed earlier, more cores don't necessarily mean better gaming so this might not be a worthwhile option – however, if you're looking to shave some of the costs off your system then switching from Intel to AMD will give you that opportunity.

It always seems like AMD is playing catch-up to Intel, but thanks to its successes in the mobile space the company has begun to shorten the distance.

Intel CPUs tend to cost more for fewer cores, but the point is that those that are included run more efficiently and effectively than AMD equivalents.

PART  # System memory

System memory or RAM is a major part of your PC build since it generally affects how quick it is at loading programs or data, and the cost can be significant with 128GB kits of DDR4 costing around £600. But that's an absolute extreme and is completely unnecessary for any but the most obsessive of tech-heads. While the memory market is in a constant state of change – as with any tech industry – there's mercifully a good bit of consistency when it comes to what works, compatibility and requirements for gaming.

There are three factors to consider: the number of modules, the capacity of the modules and the clock speed of the memory. There are hundreds of combinations of makes and models, but perhaps the starting point should be the heat spreaders. That may sound like a cosmetic point, but you need to be sure the memory will fit in your motherboard and won't interfere with a high-end air cooler. On the other hand, if you are using liquid cooling then you can be confident the heat spreaders won't pose a problem.

How much memory do you need? Truthfully, you can literally run as much memory as you can afford, but you are unlikely to gain much benefit from installing more than 16GB. There is no harm in spending the extra cash on 32GB if you really feel the speed of your system is important, but anything beyond that is just frivolous. There's

A lot of high-end RAM well suited to gaming comes with customisable RGB lighting, which is a nice extra for those who buy a PC case with a glass panel to see inside.

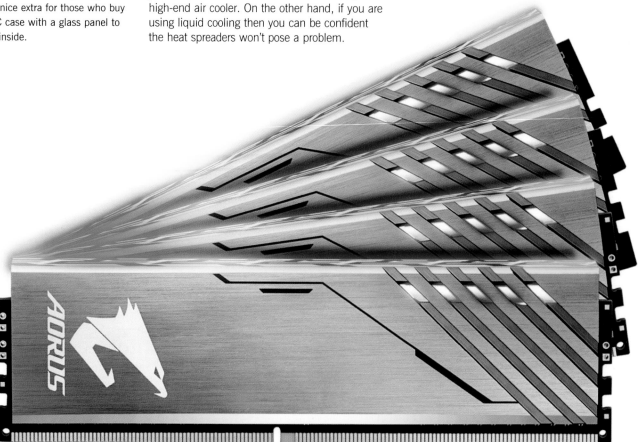

also a matter of how quickly your RAM can work – measured in MHz – but as with the maximum number of modules and their capacity, your motherboard will dictate what is possible when it comes to this.

In terms of the build, the RAM is perhaps the most flexible and the best way to add a little extra oomph at fairly low cost. For gaming, however, 8GB or 16GB will be enough; the question really comes down to what type of memory do you want?

Memory type

DIMM, DRAM, DDR, SDRAM; there are all sorts of types of memory and it can get a little overwhelming. Some types even have their own specialised acronyms for specific models – and frankly it's all a little much. DDR is the most common and easily the most reliable and compatible type to fit into a gaming PC. DDR itself has since evolved across a number of generations, with the current affordable standard being DDR4. Think of this like how new iPhones are released every year; there's always going to be a newer, faster model. What's important is picking the right one for you. Mercifully you won't find too much out of the ordinary when it comes to shopping for memory, though you will need to check with your motherboard that it is compatible. DDR4 is more affordable than ever, but some AMD chipsets are still limited to DDR4 and that will restrict the speed of the memory. If budget isn't a problem then it's certainly worth picking up a set of DDR4 memory sticks, but so long as you get a high-end DDR3 set you won't notice much difference – and your wallet will thank you too. On top of that, 2019 was the debut release of DDR5 and as such it's still bound to the higher end of the scale for those with cash to burn; until its price lowers dramatically, it won't yet be worth the advantages it offers.

Memory size

This is perhaps the most significant number to look out for when buying RAM, if only because it directly correlates to the amount of data the RAM will handle. Remember that most processors will be limited to 64GB of RAM – so don't worry too much about jamming 128GB in there – but in truth 32GB is way more than enough. If you're looking to save money on your budget then 8GB will more than suffice, but for only a little extra cost you'll be able to get 16GB instead and gain a significant advantage for doing so. There are plenty of options available, so make sure you shop around to find out what is best for you. Whatever you do, don't confuse this with your RAM's speed – memory size is simply the amount of data your RAM can handle at any one time. The higher that number the more it can do before the system begins to slow down.

Memory channel

It's imperative that you take note of the memory channel and make sure it matches up with that of your motherboard. The channel simply refers to the optimal setup for the number of individual memory sticks, and in most cases memory kits are sold as complete channel packages – often denoted by the description of the RAM itself, for example 2X8GB meaning there are two sticks of RAM in the kit. Dual channel is the most common and will likely be the one you need to pick for your motherboard, but kits can come in triple- and quad-channel too. It's worth noting that you can remove individual memory sticks from a kit and still have it function well, but for the added expense it's better to make sure you buy a channel that corresponds with your motherboard's capabilities. Additionally, while you can install quad-channel kits into a dual-channel motherboard (where space allows), it's important to know that this can lead to issues that can reduce functionality. Due to the way the motherboard may detect the memory, it may not detect the additional memory at all, its timings may be totally off (affecting system stability) and could even reduce the 'visible' memory total to a single memory unit. To avoid any problems, it's better to buy matching memory channels.

Speed and latency

The two biggest elements to affect how fast your memory works is speed (otherwise known as frequency or clock speed) and its latency. The frequency – measured in MHz and often in denominations of 1,600MHz, 1,800MHz, 2,133MHz, 2,400MHz and 3,000MHz – is a measurement of the RAM's bandwidth, and affects how much data can be moved to and from it at a time. Latency, instead, affects how quickly data can be transferred from the RAM and this can be a very confusing statistic to look up. Often seen as CAS Latency (seen as a set of numbers,

You may see memory like this that comes without any of the extras. It's cheaper, yes, but without the heat sinks installed you'll need to make efforts to reduce the running temperature of them.

Sets of memory can currently get up to 128GB across eight modules. This is a little excessive at the moment, and you'll have to make sure your motherboard can handle it.

such as 15-17-17-35), the key here is to look for lower numbers rather than higher – the opposite of many of the parts you'll be buying. This is the 'timing' of the RAM or how long between actions; the lower the time between actions, the faster that RAM will work. You'll likely spend a bit more for a CAS Latency beginning with 14 (the first number, while not the only important one, is the one to look out for).

However, usually when one of these figures improves it is at the expense of the other; your RAM may think faster, but as a result it will be able to handle less data. In truth the extra speed doesn't actually offer much in the way of performance gains, which means it's about finding that balance. If DDR4 is the RAM you're going for then a CAS Latency of 14–16 with a frequency or speed of 2400–3000 will be the best option. What's interesting, however, is that while DDR4 does have better storage density and power efficiency, it tends to have higher CAS Latency than DDR3. With everything taken

into consideration, however, DDR4 still has better overall performance.

XMP and AMP

You'll never get a stick of RAM capable of XMP and AMP – because they're both exactly the same, only AMP is the AMD version of the otherwise more common XMP. All memory as it is bought comes with its 'safe' setting, a profile that is a little below the true potential of the RAM that adjusts the timings (latency) and frequency to settings lower than it is actually capable of. This is to ensure there are few problems – since hardware can be installed on a whole range of machines, and compatibility is a manufacturer's prime concern. Nowadays many memory kits come with XM or AM profiles, in-built settings that can be manually activated to get the optimal performance out of your RAM without having to overclock it or adjust settings yourself. If this feature is present, don't be afraid to use it.

PART  Graphics cards

So far we have covered form factor, motherboards, processors and memory, yet graphics have barely merited a mention. When you consider that an NVIDIA GeForce RTX 2080 sells for the thick end of £700, it is quite easy to spend £1,400 for an SLI set-up, so graphics are a huge consideration.

Happily, unless you are deeply involved in the finer points of overclocking, we don't need to know a huge amount about the technology behind graphics cards. There are only two companies in the gaming graphics chip market, AMD (which bought ATI) and NVIDIA, who consistently leapfrog each other as they develop new graphics chips and come up with clever ideas to make gameplay better. The wonderful thing for gamers is that AMD and NVIDIA GPUs have to work with a number of important technologies and this means that modern graphics cards are interchangeable in a gaming PC, provided we install the correct driver software to allow the card to work properly. Both AMD and NVIDIA support PCI Express 3.0 and the same 6-pin and 8-pin power connectors that you find on any decent power supply, while

the display connections for hooking up to your monitor(s) are all the same, too. This means we are able to treat these competing graphics cards as a simple lump of graphics power, and don't need to worry quite so much about compatibility.

At present NVIDIA's technology trumps AMD's for efficiency and low power draw while delivering high performance, and the nature of the graphics market means that AMD has been forced to drop their prices to make up for their technological deficit. But these two companies also sell their reference cards to a whole host of manufacturing partners, and it's here that the range of GPU availability broadens out.

There are some numbers that need to be considered when buying a GPU, and naturally the more capably you want to render 3D scenes

The current top-end range from NVIDIA is its Turing series, which itself comes in three tiers of price ranges. All of them allow for some degree of ray tracing, however.

The Titan is NVIDIA's extreme end of the scale, with a single card costing over £2,000. This is really only for diehard enthusiasts with a lot of cash.

at a smooth 60 frames per second, the more the price of this piece of hardware begins to dominate the build. Most of us would be perfectly happy to buy a graphics card with 4GB of memory, although stepping into very high-resolution screens, VR or the extreme end of 120frames/sec does mean you'll want to start looking at 6GB, 8GB or even 12GB of memory. We'll ignore dual-GPU models as they are thin on the ground, awfully expensive and not much different to a pair of graphics cards in CrossFireX or SLI. Make no mistake, the GPU is a costly decision to make – but it's also one of the areas where there's quite a bit more freedom of choice, too.

Manufacturer

While there are only really two designers of GPUs – AMD and NVIDIA – there are a vast number of manufacturers, and while that might be confusing for the first-time buyer it's actually much better

for consumers since it keeps prices down and stimulates competition and innovation. As with all such things, however, some manufacturers are better than others, and that's an always-changing, dynamic system. The likes of Asus, MSI, EVGA and Gigabyte are all well-reputed for their quality products at competitive prices – you won't need to pay over the odds to get a decent GPU from one of these manufacturers. Picking a manufacturer is not an easy task, but nor is it really one we can help with – just check out some reviews of different GPUs and if they are primarily positive and talk about the graphics card's reliability and build quality then you should know it's from a trustworthy manufacturer. Just be vigilant and you should have few problems, since the better products have a tendency to rise to the top anyway.

Memory

The beauty of buying a graphics card is that, by and large, look for a large memory number from a trusted manufacturer and in all likelihood you'll have a card worth buying. That's not a hard-and-fast rule, of course, but it highlights the significance of your memory. The more memory your card has the more it'll cost since it is capable of creating even better visuals as a result. As such your budget will largely determine what size memory you can get. NVIDIA tends to dominate the market with its low-power but incredibly efficient cards that can typically outperform AMD cards with more memory. At 4GB you'll likely have no problems running most modern games – even some of the high-end ones – but it won't futureproof you by any stretch. These days 6GB and even 8GB cards tend to offer the right balance between cost and capabilities, though 11GB cards or NVIDIA's Titan with 24GB are available at prices typically out of reach for most. It's better to shop around within your budget rather than devote yourself

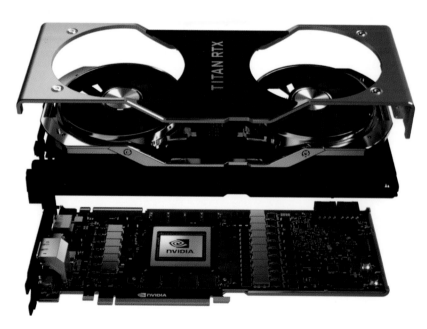

to a particular memory goal, but more is very much better when it comes to a smooth gaming experience.

Cores

This will likely confuse newcomers since many online stores advertise the number of cores as a primary feature of GPUs rather than, as we say, the size of the memory. There is some significance to it, and ultimately the number of cores tells you how speedy a particular GPU is. It's not a strict comparison that needs making since some cards can use fewer cores more efficiently or to compute more complex tasks, but it's a good value to compare all the same. The higher the number of cores the quicker that card will be able to run; of course, it's not quite as clear cut as that, but these days the number of cores is often quite comparable to a GPU's potential – so don't worry yourself too much about this aspect. As with your card's memory, instead shop within your budget rather than stressing too much about the number of cores.

Core/Boost Clock

Tying into the total number of cores is the individual core speed, and is the way in which some cards with the same number of cores (or even fewer) can be more capable than others. Imagine cores as tiny engines for your graphics card: the Core Clock speed – measured in MHz – denotes just how fast that engine can work. That means a higher figure here will denote a card whose cores can work quicker than competitors, so it's a good – albeit not imperative – measurement to consider. Boost Clock, however, is the speed that the GPU is capable of; as with all PC hardware, GPUs are sold at an underperforming rate to keep it safe for your system and for the card's longevity. While you won't need to increase that clock speed initially, it's good to take note of this number all the same – it'll help you understand its potential should you want to overclock it in the future.

Cooling

Every GPU will come with its own on-board fan, a necessary method of keeping your card cool while it's busy creating all those lovely on-screen graphics. It will be taking the brunt of the processing for 3D gaming, so keeping it cool is imperative. Manufacturers' methods and preferences for cooling changes from card to card, and in truth great strides have been made in power

consumption over the last few years so you may not need to worry too much about cooling. With that said, it's always worth spending just a little bit extra to get a card that comes with at least two on-board fans – it's just a little extra security on top of your own cooling systems to ensure your GPU is treated well. You can get cards with three fans, too, but these end up being smaller and have to work harder (and louder) as a result; and the benefits in cooling they provide aren't all that noticeable.

Power supply

Since the GPU in your PC is going to be the part that is eating up well over half of your machine's power – at least under load – you should be aware of the amount of juice you're going to need to power it. This will directly affect what power supply unit you'll need to buy, after all. Luckily the details on these cards often have both its demand and a suggested supply unit. The demand will depend entirely on the cards you're looking at and how powerful they are, but you'll be looking at the low end of 200W up to and even over 450W – though GPUs are becoming much more efficient (and therefore less power hungry). You'll actually want a power demand that is lower since that means the card will run cooler

The more fans that are on a card, naturally the cooler it will run. Depending on the ways in which you intend to cool your system, this might be important.

The GPU is undoubtedly the most important part of any gaming machine, but it doesn't need to be a high-end beast to be worthwhile.

and quieter as a result, but remember that demand is correlative to its power as a GPU, so you won't get a high-performance card with an especially low consumption rate.

SLI/CrossFire

Most dedicated gaming graphics cards offer SLI or CrossFire functionality these days, so you won't need to worry about it all that much. They're both terms for the ability to run two or more GPUs alongside one another, effectively doubling your potential graphical output (as well as the cost). It's very much a high-end method and if you want the absolutely most powerful machine then this is an option you'll want to consider – but as a result you'll need to take into account your power supply, case size, motherboard, cooling systems and even a processor capable of running it without a bottleneck. Of course, you could add an additional card in SLI/CrossFire later on, but if you're going to do it we'd recommend buying two of the same cards simultaneously to avoid any problems – technology changes all the time, and there's no guarantee you'll find a card matching yours when the time comes.

Connectivity and dimensions

Perhaps this is only a small factor in the grand scope of your GPU, but it's still important all the same. Dimensions, first and foremost, are integral since you'll want to be sure your new card actually fits. This is both its physical size – so as to fit within your case without issue – as well as the number of slots it'll take up on your motherboard. These slots will almost certainly be PCI Express (or PCIe) and for a typical gaming PC GPU it'll likely take up the space of two slots. In most situations you'll have no problems in this regard since there's a fair degree of standardisation to sizes these

days, but it's worth checking to be certain all the same. Connectivity is important, too, since it tells you through what means your GPU will display images onto your monitor. This is good to know since one affects the purchase of the other, and you'll want to know you can utilise that beast of a GPU to the very best by connecting through the best possible video cable.

Tips for picking the right GPU

We can probably guess just how you feel at this point. Graphics cards are perhaps the most important part of any gaming PC, and with so many options available it can seem a little overwhelming – even when armed with the necessary info to make a good decision. For newcomers to PC building there's always going to be a paranoid sensation that the GPU you've bought is, in some small way, inferior to another you had eyed. It's safe to ignore that sensation; that's not necessarily doubt that is talking but instead the confusion, wariness and apprehension over the cost. So long as you've come to a decision that is within your budget, provides for your gaming needs and perhaps even offers a little room for future-proofing then you should be satisfied.

But we also know that confident words of assurance won't help, so if you really need assistance prior to making that costly purchase then consider user reviews. Many websites include a rating system, while others even feature written reviews from customers, and while it's not a definite reason to trust in a purchase it will likely ease some concerns (or answer them, even) in seeing other customers explain their experiences with the graphics card. If you select a handful of potential purchases then you can use the general consensus of opinion to make your ultimate decision. It helps to look at the number of reviews available, too; if one card has a much higher number of reviews placed than another, you can safely assume that the former is much more popular and the laws of commerce suggests that this may well be the better product.

Alternatively, it's also good to use benchmarks. Numerous tech websites offer benchmark comparisons between different GPUs, whether that's a bespoke scoring system to rate and compare numerous different cards against one another or such results included as part of a professional review. Since so many different factors can alter the performance of a card, using these benchmarks can be a great way to find out which of your selected GPUs will provide the better gaming experience, and whether it might be worth altering that budget slightly for a significant gain in GPU power.

PART  Cases

Your PC case is about as close to an expression of your identity as building a PC can get, making it as much about how it looks as how it functions.

The common practice when thinking of a new PC build – especially for first-timers – is to preoccupy yourself with the machine's innards. There's so much to consider already, the case can often be seen as the fairly simple choice; away from the confusing acronyms and technical details, the housing for your gaming PC's hardware is just a protective metal chassis and little else, right? Well, there is more to it than that.

An empty case might look like it has plenty of space, but once you start jamming in dedicated coolers and dual-GPUs, this space can quickly evaporate.

More than any other aspect of building a gaming PC, the case has the widest range of options open to you. And while it can be fairly straightforward if all you're looking for is a non-descript box and follow the expectations of your motherboard's form factor, there are still details beyond the aesthetic that are significant considerations. Is there enough space for your chosen card? How many drive bays do you want or need? What are the front-panel connections? Do you want a silent case or is a little noise acceptable?

So you see, there's a lot more to consider than you might think. More than that, however, practically every question is one of preference. Unlike the technical hardware which is affected primarily by the games you want to play, much of what you want from a case is down to your

personal wants from the machine itself – including how it looks. It will perhaps take longer than any other part to come to a final decision on this simply because of this breadth of variety.

And like anything else, the cost of a case could be as little or as much as you want or can afford. Budget options are available, but you'll lose many highly demanded functions and features as a result. Spending £40 wouldn't get you anything exciting, and in truth you're at greater risk of buying something with poor design that ultimately leads to limited air flow about the case. It's a tricky balance when it comes to picking a budget for the case, so consider the following:

Case size

If you've an idea of the sort of requirements that you'll need your gaming PC to meet, then the size of the case is likely to be one of the key elements that enable that. As a result, this will affect which motherboard you can use and, from there, every other part that is connected to it. In truth, gaming PCs can easily take up a lot of physical space in a room, so if it's necessary for you to minimise the size of the PC itself then you'll need to pay particularly close attention to the dimensions. Remember to pick a motherboard that corresponds to the compatible space inside the PC – which are always in the specifications – and that while you can go incredibly small for a gaming PC, the build itself becomes much harder if you do since you'll be far more limited with what will fit inside and the need to control heat output.

Sound dampening

While the promise of a 'silent gaming PC' is a bit misleading, there are steps that can be taken to minimise the noise coming from your PC, which can be an important goal for your build if it's to share space with others while you're gaming. The case is by no means the only way to help with this, but by buying a case with sound dampening material installed onto the panels you'll find that any of the sound that your hardware makes when under load will be reduced to a tolerable amount. Some case manufacturers specialise in 'silent' cases and others might produce a case within each of their generational releases that cater to this demand, but either way a case designed for 'silent' performance will be quite clearly advertised as such.

Fans and airflow

Heat is the biggest threat to your hardware, and the more powerful you go the more you'll need to concern yourself with what to do with the heat that builds up. The simplest defence is to choose a case with a huge amount of space inside; this will allow air to more easily move about the case and therefore allow heat to dissipate better. But to take control of the matter yourself you should use ventilation to draw in cool air and remove the hot air (typically from the front and bottom and out through the top and back). Outside of the budget cases, most manufacturers offer at least a couple of fans to help keep everything cool, but stock fans aren't always enough. Knowing how much space there is for additional fans – or even water cooling if that's the route you want to take – is a pretty significant thing to look for in a case.

Ease of build

These days PC building is becoming increasingly simple thanks in large part to the standardisation of 'tool-less' chassis. These benefits aren't something that should control your purchasing decision, mostly because cases better suited to gaming are typically designed with these construction advantages in mind, but it can be enough to help you pick one option over another. While you do want to look for this benefit – essentially it means reduced risk of damaging the screws thanks to thumb screws or fasteners – there are other advantages that

Mini-ITX size cases are the trickiest builds because the space is so limited, but so long as you're smart about your purchases, then a PC this size can still pull its weight.

Some manufacturers are better at one aspect of a case than another. While you're researching what you want, you'll quickly find out what those are.

NZXT cases are well regarded for their sleek, modern design, but the manufacturer doesn't let up on the functionality features of their cases, either.

can swing things: rubber grommets to protect storage drives, custom drive bay locations or the always-useful cable management options to name just a few.

Front-panel options

This is another situation that falls down to personal preference. Most cases will come with the bare minimum of a couple of USB 3.0 ports and perhaps a headphone and microphone jack. These are useful for reducing the amount of time moving the computer to access the connections at the back, but there can be so much more. Some come with ports of SD cards or Thunderbolt 3, volume and individual fan controls, and even LCD displays for monitoring heat. Not only that, but how the front panel is designed can be a significant feature, too, since some will hide the buttons and ports away from view behind doors or on the top of the case, while others are intended to be a lot flashier with LED lighting. Since this is the part of the machine that you'll usually be looking at the most, it's not a decision to be taken lightly.

PART

Power, storage and cooling

At this point we've covered pretty much the core hardware of any gaming PC, which is to say those parts that will have an effect on the actual gaming itself. But by no means can you count the job finished, since there are still other crucial parts of any computer that need to be considered. Luckily there's not so many technical aspects to worry yourself with when it comes to these remaining needs.

Power supply units

There are certain considerations that you'll need to be aware of when it comes to buying a PSU, and the number one is that it will provide enough power to keep everything running smoothly. Your GPU will likely offer a suggested power supply guideline, so that's your first port of call. Next is your CPU, which is perhaps the second biggest power demand in a gaming PC. All told you can expect a PSU of between 450W and 650W to be enough to keep your machine powered for a single-GPU build.

But that's not all, because a better-quality PSU can be the best insurance you can buy for your computer. Remember, this is the part of the machine that takes AC power and distributes it safely around all that expensive hardware; a fault here can be a costly catastrophe. A good quality PSU will not only last you longer and can be run at or around its limit without much fear of a fault, but if you buy one that's 100W or so higher than your current need then you'll be able to easily repurpose it for the next build.

But what you really want is to buy an

The power supply you choose will have a serious effect on the longevity of all of your computer's parts.

While SSD used to be prohibitively expensive, it has come down in price in recent years to mean that it's worth the cost to take advantage of the speedier read times.

efficient power supply. Without getting into the gritty details too much, an efficient PSU more effectively converts input AC into output DC for the computer's hardware, meaning that there is less wasted energy. In the long run this results in lower energy bills for running your gaming rig, but in the short term it means that there's less heat pumped out by the PSU into the case and therefore your system's internal heat won't be affected too dramatically – and heat reduction is crucial to the longevity of your hardware. With this in mind, only buy a PSU rated in the 80 Plus scheme. This guarantees an efficiency of at least 80%, with ratings covering Bronze, Silver, Gold, Platinum, and

Titanium; the higher the grade the more pricey the PSU will be, but it's a solid investment to spend a little extra here.

The last thing to think about is what's known as 'modular cabling', a means by which the power supply can have all unused cables removed to clear up space and clutter within the case. They're a lovely bonus that you will pay a little more for, but it's entirely optional and is only really worth considering if you're particular about keeping the inside of the case clutter free.

Storage

When it comes to storage, the industry is fairly consistent. There are always new innovations for faster and more secure storage options, and those are typically the most expensive purchases. Hard disk drives (HDD) have been around for decades, physically write data onto a storage medium and are the cheapest options available. Solid-state drives have been around for a while too, but are much quicker and are still going through evolution. On top of that there are M.2 SSD options, which are increasingly popular and are installed directly onto the motherboard with a much smaller form factor. While M.2 connections are quicker than their SATA SSD drive equivalents, the difference between load times aren't so significant to be the primary reason to opt for this version, however the prices between the two aren't often that different – in fact most manufacturers will offer either option as part of a particular model of SSD at pretty much the same price.

While solid-state drives have become much more affordable in recent years, they're still limited in terms of both size and price. Since installing a large number of games can easily chew through a terabyte of data, it's unfeasible for most of us to kit out a machine entirely in

Increasingly M.2 SSD drives are becoming more popular inside gaming PCs, which offer negligible read times over SATA SSD but are installed directly into the motherboard.

SSD storage. So what most people tend to do is to equip the machine with both types: 250GB or 500GB of quicker SSD storage for the installation of the operating system and regularly accessed programs and games, and 2TB or 3TB of standard hard drive storage for all those games. You could probably spend a little less on just a single 1TB solid-state drive than this combo, but then you're more likely to encounter situations of having to balance which games you want installed. It's a preferential thing and you'll easily find a balance that fits your needs, but the beauty of storage is that it's one of those few parts of computer hardware that can be upgraded as and when you need to.

Of course, since all your data will be stored on these drives, you'll want to make sure the one you're buying is trusted. We can't entirely help with this, though purchasing a Samsung, Western Digital, Crucial or Seagate drive is more likely to offer a degree of security. As ever, user reviews will be your friend here.

Cooling

When it comes to cooling your gaming PC, you have two options open to you: air ventilation with fans or an all-in-one liquid cooler. The difference is significant, since one draws the hot air through the middle of your case and out through exhaust fans at the back or top while the other transfers the produced heat directly to the radiator at the edge of the case where it is

dissipated immediately into the cool air outside of the case. The latter naturally sounds much better, but the trickiness of installing an AIO cooler, the risk that comes with having water so close to your computer's innards and the higher cost means it's certainly worthwhile considering alternatives. For one, the radiators take up much more space than a couple of fans, and if you're not overclocking any of your parts then actually it should be sufficient to add fans into the system to get the job done cheaply and just as effectively.

The fact of the matter is, liquid cooling is often seen as the end goal for an enthusiast PC builder purely for its complicated and risky nature. Absolute beginners likely aren't looking to reach this Holy Grail straight away, especially since the likes of dual-GPU setups and overclocking probably isn't on their mind. There's already a lot to think about when it comes to building your first gaming PC, so why make it more complex than it needs to be, especially when air cooling is more than enough for standard single-GPU systems?

Regardless of your choice, there's a certain amount of standardisation to help you make a decision, this tying into the available space of your case. Typically a PC case will have a certain allotment of space divided into 120mm, 140mm, 240mm, 280mm and finally 360mm spaces for fans and radiators; how these are divvied up is entirely down to you.

Ensuring your gaming PC runs coolly is extremely important, but liquid cooling isn't automatically the best option for every system.

PART  **Build a gaming PC**

Hopefully by this point you've done all the research you can and picked out a set of components you're happy to use for your very first gaming PC. If so, it's onto the next nail-biting step: putting everything together. It's understandable if you feel a bit of apprehension; this is the moment of truth, in a way. But believe us when we say, it's not nearly as difficult as it might seem. You need to take care, of course, but for the most part everything is going to slot together nicely.

Before we jump into the step-by-step process, however, we're going to layout our build. This shouldn't be considered tips for your own build (if you've learnt anything about this so far, it should be that PC building is a truly personal experience), but it will be helpful to understand our reasoning since that will guide some of the construction process.

The Fractal Define S completely forgoes the traditional drive bays to really open up the internal space of the case. It's a great silent case for customisation.

• Fractal Design Define S Mid Tower	**£75**
• Gigabyte Intel Z390 UD motherboard	**£105**
• Intel i7 9700K 3.60GHz CPU	**£385**
• Gigabyte NVIDIA GeForce GTX 1660 6GB graphics card	**£230**
• Corsair Vengeance LPX CL16 16GB DDR4 RAM	**£70**
• Crucial MX500 1TB 3D NAND M.2 SSD	**£110**
• Fractal Design R3 Silent Case Fan 120mm	**£10**
• Be Quiet! 600W Pure Power 11 CM 80 Plus Gold PSU	**£75**
• Cooler Master Hyper 212X Tower CPU Cooler	**£25**
• Gigabyte Combo Intel 11ac Wireless Network Card	**£25**
TOTAL COST	**£1,105**

We could have very easily thrown stacks of cash at our hypothetical build and still explain everything in the following guide, but where's the fun in that? As we explained in the chapter about researching your computer, it's good to have a goal in mind when coming up with what parts you need in your gaming PC – and that's exactly what we did. Sure, we could've conceived our dream build, but that wouldn't have been realistic for a large number of the readers of this book. Our goal, then, was to build a gaming PC that could comfortably handle the latest high-end games with an eye for VR capabilities, while still keeping within a modest budget. We also wanted to design a PC that was going to run quietly, because in our imagined home we expected it to sit in the corner of the living room and so couldn't ring out the decibels too much.

That last point ended up being a defining feature, in fact. It meant we opted for the Fractal Design Define S tower, one of the top cases when it comes to sound dampening while a number of ease-of-build features helped to make it a solid choice. There's no option for optical drives, for example, which isn't quite as drastic as it might seem. It might not be the most attractive case out there and certainly wouldn't impress any guests like the NZXT case we were eyeing up, but for our goal it was perfect.

There were compromises, however. To keep within a modest budget we chose not to spend as much as we would've liked on the GPU. The GTX 1660 OC is a mainstream card for NVIDIA's impressive Turing-powered GPUs, and while we could've spent a bit more on its boosted Ti version, our choice here is still capable of 1080 at 60FPS for the majority of the biggest PC games. It's here that our system had to take the biggest hit, but it's by no means held back. The real secret is that this is one of the coolest-running and quietest 6GB GPUs at the moment, which helped make it a more tempting pick for our particular build. For the money, this is one of the best cards around.

In seeking silence, we also went a little showy on storage by opting for a full terabyte of M.2 SDD storage. This removes any moving parts in the storage drive and that, therefore, means less noise. As ever with storage, there's always options to expand if it was necessary, and the novel storage drive bays that come with the Define S case mean that if it did come to that we wouldn't be too impacted by where and how it fits into the machine.

You may also notice that we opted simply for two relatively cheap fans rather than any major aftermarket cooler. It's true that liquid cooling systems are quieter, but Fractal's efforts in quiet running systems are well known and its Silent R3 fan will do the job of quietly getting hot air out of the machine through the top of the case. The addition of a solid, dedicated CPU cooler means that we won't have to worry too much

The 1660 OC (meaning overclocked) is a great card that finds a perfect balance between affordability, cool and quiet operation, and is still capable of VR and high-end graphics.

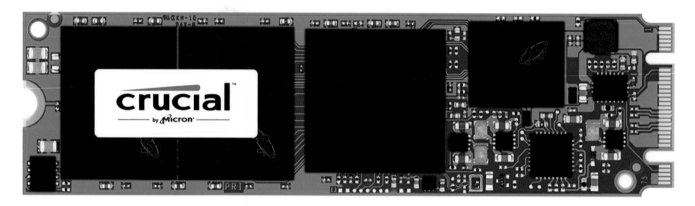

There are a number of advantages when it comes to an M.2 storage drive, but if a terabyte ends up not being enough it's easy to expand.

We purposefully chose a GPU that ran relatively coolly, but the CPU can't fend for itself. By using this hefty CPU fan we'll be able to overclock the processor without issue.

about the processor having issues. This is partly why we spent a bit more on the PSU, opting for a Be Quiet product – a company that is well known for its quality without stiffing customers on the price. The significant detail here is the 80 Plus Gold rating, which means greater efficiency and therefore reduced heat being pumped into the machine itself. Combine this with the cool-running GPU and there shouldn't be much need for more cooling to be added to our build.

This is a machine that would see us comfortably into the future, with the parts that aren't so easy to swap out for improved picks having a little more spent on them to ensure they'll last the whole hog. We could've easily spent a good chunk more on aspects like the CPU and the GPU to really guarantee the stable 60 frames per second that is optimal for PC gamers, but we challenged ourselves to find a balance between affordability and performance, just to prove it could be done. We could also have chosen to reduce the costs further, and if you're on an even stricter budget or are happy with 30 frames per second, then there's scope to reduce the cost still.

As for the build itself, well we've arranged it into a fashion that is easier to find the part you're hoping to install. You'll want to follow the order if you're starting from scratch, but we've categorised each part should you want to retrace your steps. Where we can we've provided alternatives for particular parts or case layouts, but you'll need to be aware of any potential differences with your own equipment. All cases and parts are different and so we can't give an exact run down, but with these steps you'll have no problem tackling whatever situation you find yourself in.

PART **3** Installing the CPU

Prepare the case

The worst first move would be to screw your motherboard into the case without first installing the most important – not to mention delicate – components of the entire system. Start by taking the panels off the case of the PC, typically through two thumbscrews at the back of the case on either side. Then remove the motherboard from its packaging and rest it on a sturdy, well-lit table.

Unlock the CPU socket

There are either one or two levers on either side of the CPU socket; push down and away from the socket on these one by one to release them. Pull them up and clear of the socket. This will release the load plate, which in turn can be lifted to free the CPU socket's protective cover. Note the four alignment keys on the naked socket in all four corners and the triangular mark in one of the corners.

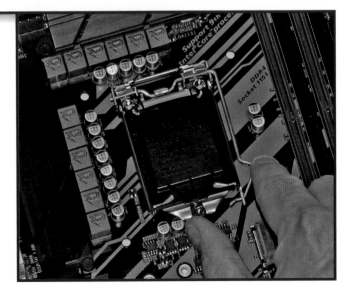

Install the processor

The alignment keys and the triangular mark are mirrored on the processor. Orientate the processor so the triangular mark is in the same place and – without touching the metal contacts on either the processor or the motherboard – gently place the processor into the socket. It will fit very snugly, but if it doesn't appear to be sat correctly, lift it to reposition it (don't be tempted to simply wiggle it around where it lies).

Secure the socket

Once you're happy the processor is sat squarely on the socket, carefully lower the load plate, which is designed to ensure no one side or corner of the processor takes too much pressure when the cooler is installed later on. Next lower and secure the levers on both sides of the processor. It takes a reasonable amount of force so don't be too shy.

PART # Installing a CPU cooler

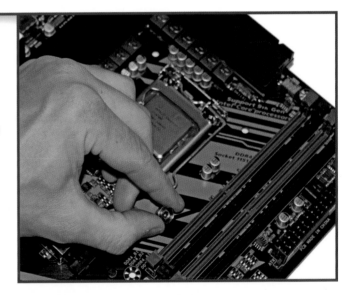

Prepare the mounting plate

Air coolers can come in countless shapes and sizes, but larger ones will always come with a mounting plate that is attached to the back of the motherboard. This balances the weight of the heavy cooler, which will be held horizontally in the machine. Start this by placing the holders into each of the holes at the corners of the CPU. You might need to do this and the next step four separate times.

Attach the mounting plate

Position the plate into position on the back of the motherboard, using the notches in the corner to align the correct position. These plates are designed to fit multiple motherboards, but will only have a position where each of the holes align properly. Attach the nut to each of the holders, securing the mounting plate onto the back.

Tightening the nuts

You'll have to make sure that this mounting plate is very securely attached, since these cooling fans are pretty heavy. The methods can differ from model to model, but in most cases you'll be provided with a cap that can be used to screw the nuts more tightly. You'll then need to flip over the motherboard and line up the cross-shaped grip with the corresponding positions of the holders.

Attach the grip

Don't secure the grip in place just yet since there's a crucial step that is needed beforehand. Try positioning the two in place with a dry run, then once you've found the right spot where everything aligns properly, attach the central screw of the grip onto the central point of the cooler's base. This will be the part that holds the cooler tightly onto the fan.

Apply the thermal paste

Before attaching the cooler comes the scary part: the thermal paste. Wipe clean the top of the attached CPU; usually you'll be provided with a wipe with your cooler, but if not then use isopropyl alcohol and a clean wipe to remove any dust and dirt from the top of the CPU. Then apply a very small amount of thermal paste to only the centre of the CPU; the idea is that the cooler will spread the paste for you. This is a step you may need to do again if you replace the fan, CPU or find the processor is overheating inexplicably.

Secure the cooler

Gently sit the cooler onto the CPU socket, lining up the screw holes on the mount with the screw holes on the cooler itself. Now securely fasten the cooler to the mount with a cross-headed screwdriver. Next fit the CPU fan connector to the top left of the CPU socket and then gently clip the fan mount to the flat side of the cooler, minding the blades as you go (they're both sharp and delicate).

BUILD A GAMING PC

Installing memory and M.2 storage

Locate the memory bays
Though the long black and grey memory bays are often located to the immediate right of the CPU, in many cases there can be parallel bays on either side of the processor or they could even more rarely be located above or below. Either way, find them and push down the plastic nodes that stick up on either side of the bays.

Slot in each memory module
Installing RAM is a very simple process: just line up the little notch in the middle of the RAM with the corresponding bump in the memory bay, then push down firmly on either side until you hear a satisfying 'click'. If you're not filling all of your motherboard's memory bays just yet, then the only tricky part comes down to knowing which bays you should use. For that, refer to your motherboard manual.

Locate the M.2 space

Depending on your motherboard, you may have one or more M.2 storage and – if so – you may have decided to utilise this for the speedy SSD read times that comes from the storage type. These slots can be tricky to find because the actual connection itself is quite small (the drive lies flat, parallel to the motherboard). A screw will likely be installed in one of the nodes, which each have numbers corresponding to the different sizes of M.2 drive compatible with this particular slot and the motherboard in general.

Install the M.2 drive

Unscrew the screw from the node and put it to one side. Push the M.2 drive into the connection at roughly a 30-degree angle. As with the RAM, there's only one way that the drive will go in, so if it isn't cooperating, don't force it in but instead flip it around and try again. Once connected, push the drive down (it will want to spring up again by itself) and then replace the screw at the left-hand end of the drive into the node to hold it in place.

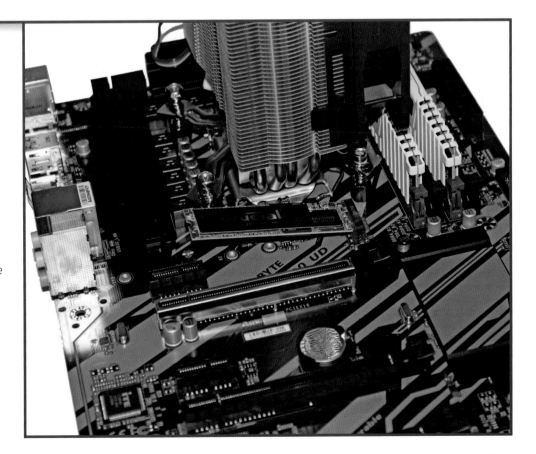

PART Fitting the motherboard

Attach the I/O shield

The first step of getting your motherboard in place is the easiest: simply take out the I/O shield that will protect all the connections at the back of your computer and slot it into place. There are little bumps on these shields that will grip onto the case, so it's just a case of aligning it and slotting it into place. There may already be something in place with your case, which you may or may not need to use.

Install the metal studs

Many modern cases have a small stud towards the centre of where the motherboard sits that allows you to hang it in place with the case stood upright. This is convenient, but not necessarily the case in all cases. If not, locate the small holes found on the back of the case and screw in each of the metal studs provided with the case.

3

Secure the motherboard
These studs are what the motherboard will sit on, separating them from the metallic back of the case and preventing electrical shorting. You may not need all of these screws, since it depends on both your case and your motherboard. Either way, position the motherboard over the studs by finding the corresponding holes. Tightly fasten the motherboard onto these studs, which can be a challenge in corners.

4

Installing horizontally
Securing the motherboard is one of the harder tasks just because it needs to be tightly secured (naturally it'll be holding all those expensive parts in place). If you're struggling to get those corner screws in properly because there isn't much space at the top of the case with the huge CPU cooler installed, then consider carefully lifting the PC up. So long as the majority of the screws are in place, you should find it easier.

5

Optional fans
If you've decided to go for some additional case fans to remove the hot air inside the machine, then now is probably the best time to install them. Some cases will come with covers for when the fan slots aren't in use, but for the most part these things are fairly modular: just pick the place you want the fan, find the holes for the screws and attach it to the case.

PART ③ Installing both hard drives

Locate the storage bays

Perhaps the most flexible part of the design of a PC case is the storage bays. Not only can these be many in number, but they can appear in all sorts of weird and wonderful places. Often that can even be detached and installed elsewhere in the case, for true custom builders. In our case, the Define S, there are no traditional drive bays but rather cases that can be detached from the back panel to secure the storage drives you want. In any case, you'll want to first find out where and how your case is utilising storage bays, and decide how you want to install your solid-state hard drives.

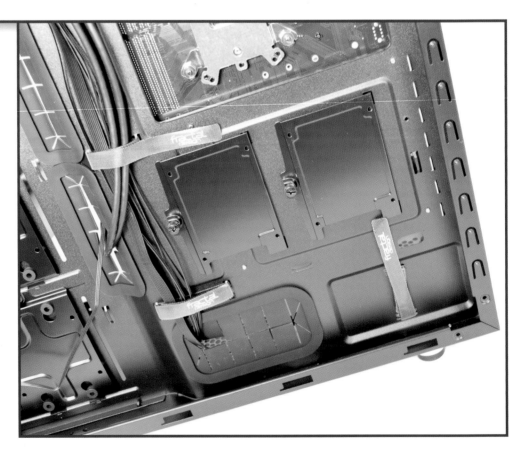

② Install the storage drive

Regardless of the type of storage you want to install or the way your case would prefer you did it, all modern cases will have a fairly simple, singular screw or thumbscrew to first provide access to the drive bay and, later, to secure the drive into the slot. Remove the screw to loosen access, then slot the drive into place. With our build, we had to attach the drive onto the detached bay, but it's fairly unique in this manner. If there's any confusion, your case manual will have all the details on this.

③ Powering the motherboard

In the majority of cases you'll be connecting your storage drive via SATA. It's a good idea to do this now, so find the part of the motherboard that says 'SATA', likely in a grid of connections. The number of these and where they are differ from motherboard to motherboard, but in most cases you'll find it along the right-hand edge of the motherboard. The connections here are fairly easy to make and fool-proof in their design, so connect up each of your drives individually and that should be all you need to do.

PART 3 Fitting a graphics card

Unscrew the PCIe slot covers
Despite being the most exciting piece of hardware during the build process, fitting the graphics card is surprisingly unexciting. Most graphics carda are double-height models these days, so remove the two PCIe slot covers from the back of the case with a screwdriver and keep onto the screws. Be careful to detach the correct covers, since it may be that another slot type – for example an M.2 slot as with our case here – actually takes up the top space and won't need to be removed.

Attach the GPU

It should be fairly obvious which way around the GPU should go, but just to be sure: make sure that the output connections are facing out of the back of the case, since you'll need access to this. Line up the GPU so that it is in the corresponding space, being sure to check that the PCIe connection – the row of pins that run along closest to the motherboard – will correctly and safely lock into place as you push on the GPU. As with the memory, a little locking mechanism should 'click' into place.

Secure the GPU

Take those screws that were holding the PCIe covers in place and reattach them to their original place, this time securing the graphics card into place. This is important because while the PCIe bay can hold onto the connector, the weight of a hefty GPU will put strain on the hardware and eventually lead to damage. Even motherboards that come with metal-bound PCIe slots to protect against this aren't really doing much to actually avoid this issue from happening.

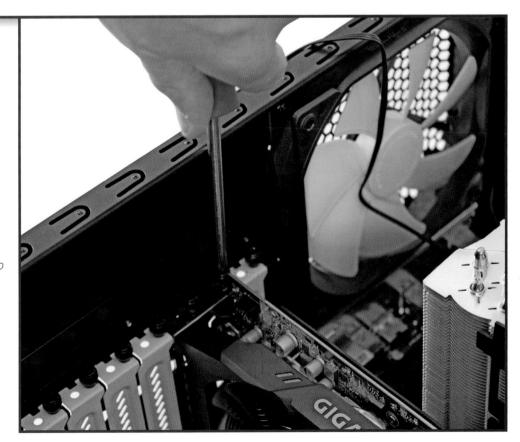

PART 3 # Installing the power supply

 Fix backing plate

Spin the case around to its rear edge. In some cases you'll have an empty space ready for your power supply, in others you'll have a backing plate that is designed to connect to the power supply itself before sliding back into the case. If that's the case, remove the backing plate, unbox your PSU and connect the plate using the four screws. Otherwise, just slot the PSU into place.

Secure the PSU into place

If you don't have one of these backing plates, then you'll most certainly need to secure the PSU into its place with the screws provided. Since power supply manufacturers handle this in a range of ways, there are a number of potential holes to use to do this. Find the ones that work for your case and PSU combination, and tightly secure it into place.

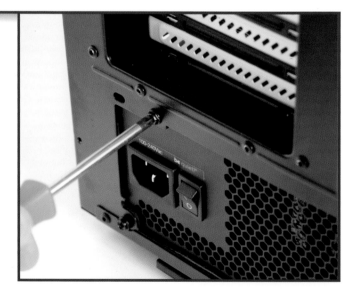

Connecting the power

When connecting the PSU's cables to the various hardware of the machine, it's important to follow the instructions supplied with your motherboard. Not only will this make it easier to follow which connections are where, but it'll mean you don't inadvertently misplace a connection. First we need to separate the large 24-pin cable and the smaller 8-pin CPU power cable from the PSU cable bundle and feed them around to their required locations. In most gaming cases you'll have a space for poking the cables through to the back, which helps keep the hardware cable-free and, as a result, better able to spread cooling air around the machine.

Connect the front panel cables

Since all the connectors for the front panel of the PC run along the very bottom edge of the motherboard, you'll want to bring them through the bottom slots if they aren't already. Again, follow the instructions with your manual to help match up the front panel elements – these help to control the LEDs and power and reset functionality of the buttons on the front of the case. There will also be a connectivity key in the motherboard manual, but be sure to get the positive and negative of each connection in the right place.

Connect the case fans

You should already have connected the CPU cooler to its corresponding connection on the motherboard, but if not then now is a good time to do so. It's also a good time to connect your case fans – including any optional ones you might have installed – to the motherboard, which isn't always easy depending on the motherboard. The cables for fans can be a little short, so smart balancing while ensuring all the wires aren't obstructing anything is crucial.

Connecting the graphics card power

One of the final PSU-related tasks is to connect the graphics card with its specific power connectors. The power of your graphics card will dictate whether it needs one or two PCIe power cables fed through the bottom cable port. We're using a pretty high-end card here so we'll need both.

PART ③ Cable routing

Keep your case tangle-free

With some cases you'll see above, below and to the side of the motherboard a number of holes between the motherboard side of the case and the side panel. It's a relatively slim cavity but there is enough room to route most of your gaming PC's cables. It's important to keep as much of the central cavity as free from cabling as possible so cool air has a clean path over your core components. Let's start by feeding through and connecting the cables for audio and USB that sit on the top of the case.

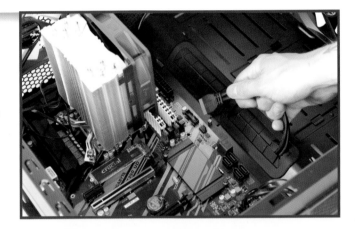

Case features

The more high-end your case is, the more attention will have been paid to cable management. As mentioned, keeping the central space as clutter-free as possible is integral to a healthy machine since it means air can move around the case more easily and heat can dissipate better. In most this amounts to spaces around the back of the motherboard for your cables, but others will include cable management options – like our Fractal Design case and its easy-to-use cable straps. Be sure to use all your case features available: we say again, good cable management is important.

Modular PSU management

We haven't really talked about the difference between modular and non-modular PSUs during installation, but you should have noticed the difference if you bought the former. Modular PSUs allow you to install only those connections that you need, so if you only need one GPU powered then you'll only need to connect one GPU power cable to the PSU. This is worth the extra cost for less clutter in your case, but if you went for a non-modular one then your last step should be to tidy up all the unused cables and use a cable tie to bundle them together. Keep them poked in a corner as far from the hardware as possible.

4

PART 4 The first start-up

Congratulations! If you've followed our guide then at this point you should have your very own gaming PC put together and ready to go. Well done you. Before you start celebrating too much, however, it's fair to say that much of the work is yet to come. Hopefully you've enjoyed the experience of putting the hardware together, but now the time has come to check the machine works and, if it does, start tinkering with the software side of things. And truth be told, as necessary as it is, that part isn't nearly as fun.

The initial start-up of your first ever gaming PC can be quite intimidating; it's the reward for your patience and effort, and if it doesn't boot up it's hard not to feel like something of a failure. But it does happen to the best of us, with common problems such as putting power connections in the wrong place stifling many a would-be powerhouse PC. Fear not, crack open that panel and have a tinker – ensure that the power is taken out, of course – and look for any connections that aren't in the right spot. If needs be, remove the PSU connections and repeat that process for each of the PC's parts in turn, using your motherboard's manual as a reference guide. Each motherboard and case is different, so it could be a simple problem you've overlooked.

But since troubleshooting can be such a large undertaking – especially if it's something greater than a misplaced power connection – we'll focus on that in a separate section later on in the book. Instead this chapter will assume all is hunky dory with your PC build, and will talk you through some of the key facets of your gaming PC post-build. It'll focus on things like installing an operating

system, booting up your PC for the first time and some of the first actions you'll want to take. It's your PC, ultimately, so you should feel free to tailor the software to match your interests or personal desires – but we'll guide you through some of the more important gaming software.

The irony is, of course, to install an operating system you'll first need access to another computer. If you can't visit a friend or go to the library then there are ways around this, but we'll talk about all that in this chapter. After everything is installed there's a temptation to jump straight into playing games – and there's certainly nothing stopping you doing that – but with just a little bit of extra work you can be completely set up without any concerns that might rear their head because you were overeager in rushing to play games. There are various settings you can tailor to make your gaming PC a truly carefree kit, so we'll detail some of these, too.

Simply put, everything that comes after the hardware installation will be discussed here and so, with only a little bit of extra work, you'll be ready and raring to go before long.

PART  Picking an operating system

We have to admit, these days it can often feel like there aren't many options when it comes to operating systems. So prevalent is Microsoft's Windows OS that it's rare many will even consider other alternatives – but they are there, with some that you might not have considered beforehand.

Since the majority of games run on 64-bit architecture (don't worry about that too much), you'll need to opt for Windows 10 if you want to go the Microsoft route.

Currently there are only really three major operating systems: Windows, OS X (exclusively for Apple Mac products) and the open-source Linux. Since you'll be running a PC you won't be able to consider OS X, reducing your core options down to only two. Windows is the simplest option of them all, not because it's the best option or even the most stable but simply because it's so commonplace. Microsoft's operating system is stable, relatively hassle-free and will have the widest possible compatibility

with games and software. But it will cost you more money, and a licence for the latest copy of Windows can add a good chunk on top of your overall budget. Windows 10 is the most recent version, allows for the true hardware potential of your system to be available to the OS and is the only way to allow for the latest version of Microsoft's API that allows for the very best of 3D graphics technology, DirectX 12, to work smoothly on Windows.

Linux is open source, meaning it is free

Mint is perhaps the Linux distro that is closest to Windows in terms of functionality and design, and offers a nice, sleek interface.

to download and install – a great option if you're looking to save some pennies. But it is worth noting that Linux does come with some issues: for one thing it won't be totally familiar to anyone who has used a PC in the last decade – this isn't Windows and you will need to learn a few things. It also has a number of compatibility issues and while it isn't quite as major an issue as it used to be, there could be concern that something – whether it's specific software you want to use or hardware and their

drivers – won't work. It's also worth noting that there are a wide range of Linux distributions or distros – a term used to describe the different 'flavours' of operating system. For each of these Linux remains the foundation, but the creator (or creators) have provided their own preference or spin on things. This can confuse matters for those looking for a new operating system, but sticking with the more popular distros – such as Ubuntu or Linux Mint – will minimise any of that hassle.

PART 4 Windows versus Linux

With a huge majority of the market share, Windows is by far and away the most popular operating system for PCs the world over. What this means is that we're fairly confident that you'll be able to pick up any model of Windows for your PC and have few problems adapting to it – even if you haven't used a PC for five years or more! That's going to take precedence if you're not willing to learn more technical elements, and we'll acknowledge that. However, we wouldn't be doing our job if we didn't at least give you the alternatives. Here's a comparison between Windows and Linux, to find out which is for you.

	Windows	Linux
Price	At a cost of around £100 for the basic licence, and up to £200 or more for more 'professional' packages, the cost of Windows can add a lot to the already expensive cost of your PC. Don't worry about shelling out for the seemingly enhanced 'Professional' versions, however, it's not likely to benefit you.	Since the majority of Linux distributions are completely free to download, the obvious winner when it comes to price is this operating system. Remember that this doesn't need to be a permanent choice; if you find you don't enjoy using your installed operating system then you can easily switch it out at a later date.
Compatibility (Software)	This is the ultimate strength of Windows, at least when it comes to games. With its huge market share, it's unsurprising that developers will first focus on a Windows version of the game, with Mac's OS X coming next and Linux after that. If playing every game as and when they come out is important to you then Windows will likely have to be the choice of OS.	Once upon a time Linux struggled when it came to game releases; very few were released on the platform and it was a sore point for many gamers. Nowadays, however – as the popularity of Linux continues to rise – it is becoming a much more viable platform for games. It doesn't hold a torch to Windows in this regard, but these days each new release is usually brought over to Linux – albeit not always simultaneously with Windows.
Compatibility (Hardware)	We'll be saying this a lot, but Windows is the most popular operating system and so, as a result, it is also more likely to receive driver support from hardware manufacturers. It's unlikely you'll have many problems with your hardware as a result of using Windows.	Manufacturers have made great strides in providing driver support for Linux, and since technical savvy gamers are – by a large margin – some of the more common users of Linux, the need to create compatible drivers for specialised PC gaming hardware means it's increasingly less rare to find your support for the expensive parts in your machine. It's still worth checking, though.
Ease of use	Since Windows is by far and away the most popular platform when it comes to PCs, the ease of use of its software is something that Microsoft has tried to focus on. Most people will know how to use a Windows PC – even with the most basic tasks – and in that regard Windows wins out when it comes to intuitiveness.	The ease of use with Linux is dependent primarily on the distribution being used. The more popular distros like Ubuntu, Mint and Debian all offer a user interface that is very familiar to Windows users, but many of the options and settings are in different places. If you're technically minded and don't mind an initial learning phase, then it's not like Linux is unintuitive by its very nature.

	Windows	Linux
Software	Windows comes with a whole host of extra bits of software – and some would say far too much of it. In truth there is a lot of bloatware inside even the basic Windows install, though there are a number of accessibility and system options available that just have no equivalent in Linux. However, these days there's often a free tool that can be downloaded for very specific needs.	Linux relies on a particular distribution to quantify just how many extra utilities and software packages come bundled with an install. Some are purposefully more svelte in this regard, while others bundle in as much as they can. It all comes down to preference, but the majority of 'essential' utilities are often all there. With Linux, however, it's far easier to install additional utilities and software completely free.
Performance	Windows is certainly a user-friendly operating system, but it's not exactly quick. A fresh install on your brand-new PC might seem pretty nippy, but after numerous mandatory updates and behind-the-scenes software running at start-up, it can soon start to make the OS run slowly. There's more manual maintenance needed to keep Windows running optimally.	Since Linux has a smaller CPU demand on the whole, the operating system itself isn't intruding on your everyday use. It's impossible to objectively compare the two since elements such as performance are affected as much by the software you install as anything else. But on average, Linux beats Windows when it comes to speed of use as it has a much lower demand on your system and less of an eagerness for bloatware.
Security	While popularity does have something to do with the amount of potential attacks to a Windows computer, the real issue is the way Windows handles access to its files and folders. If you don't make a concerted effort to protect yourself, you'll be at a bigger risk.	On a foundational level, Linux distros tend to offer greater security than Windows. Part of this is because Linux isn't nearly as popular, but the way that Linux handles administration rights (by default all users have restricted access) means that if a virus does manage to get through, the damage it can actually cause is lessened.
OS flexibility	Since Windows is a product managed, maintained and sold by Microsoft, you won't have much input over the form, function and control of the different parts of the OS. It's not likely to be a concern to most people, admittedly, but some will want the flexibility of Linux.	With Linux you not only have myriad choices of which distribution you prefer and want to use, but you have much greater control over the functions of your machine. It requires a greater technical knowledge – or, at least, a willingness to learn – but if you like the idea of being able to control everything in your OS then Linux is the way to go.

Windows has DirectX 12 and Linux has Vulkan, but due to the popularity of the former OS, it's DirectX that gets the majority of the support from developers. The latest version enables complicated terms like raytracing, variable rate shading and new antialiasing techniques in the latest games, which is to say it makes them look more realistic.

PART  Installing the OS

You might be surprised how easy it is to install an operating system. These days it's pretty much a case of getting hold of the files you need, creating what is known as a 'boot disc' then powering up the PC with it available for the BIOS to detect. This could take the form of a CD, DVD or USB. It's likely the latter will be the option you go for, but the process is essentially the same anyway.

For our guide we'll assume that you're going to opt for Windows, since it is the more popular choice and requires less technical knowledge. Since there are so many distros for Linux it's perhaps better to suggest that, whichever you go for, make sure you follow any supplied guidelines. It'll likely be just as simple, but there are far too many options for us to account for every single eventuality here.

To begin the process of installing the operating system you're going to want to first pick your method, and make sure you have the necessary hardware capabilities to do so; there's no sense preparing a boot disc on CD if you chose not to have a CD drive in your PC build!

It's also worth noting that you'll need access to the internet to download the files you need, and understandably without an operating system installed your PC won't yet be ready to do so. See if you can ask a friend if you can borrow their computer, head to the local library and use theirs or maybe even ask the IT guy at the office – you never know, maybe a pleasant smile and a chocolate chip muffin will be enough to persuade him. Anyway, let's get started:

Prepare the boot disc

If you bought a boxed copy of Windows then that's the biggest worry out of the way; it'll come with everything you need, including

There will be a waiting period while installing Windows, so feel free to go grab a cup of tea.

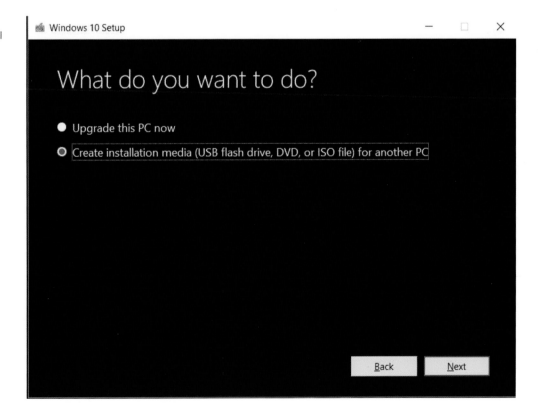

There's not all that much difference between the different versions of Windows – aside from the price – but it's good to know what is and isn't included in case you miss out on something crucial to your needs.

specific instructions on how to install the software and your associated serial key – go ahead and pop that into your CD drive, you'll be up and running in no time. If you bought a digital version from the Microsoft website – or had to download a bootable disc file since you no longer have your original disc – then that is where you need to actually create the boot disc yourself.

If you're creating your boot disc yourself then you've purchased a digital licence for Windows – it's essentially the same but without the box and removable media. Here you'll be given two options to download, either an ISO file or a collection of compressed files. You're going to want to pick the ISO file, since this

will allow you to create the boot disc. With this file downloaded, simply copy it onto a USB or DVD. With a DVD you'll need to make sure the computer you're using allows you to burn DVDs, but in truth you're likely much better sticking to USB anyway – it's quicker, easier and less permanent. Whichever you choose to go for, that's all there is to it – there's your boot disc.

Start the PC up

The next process is simple: either plug in your USB or place the DVD into the DVD tray and then boot up your PC with the power button. We're assuming you've turned your PC on once, at least, so you know it works, so this time around the BIOS will automatically detect the

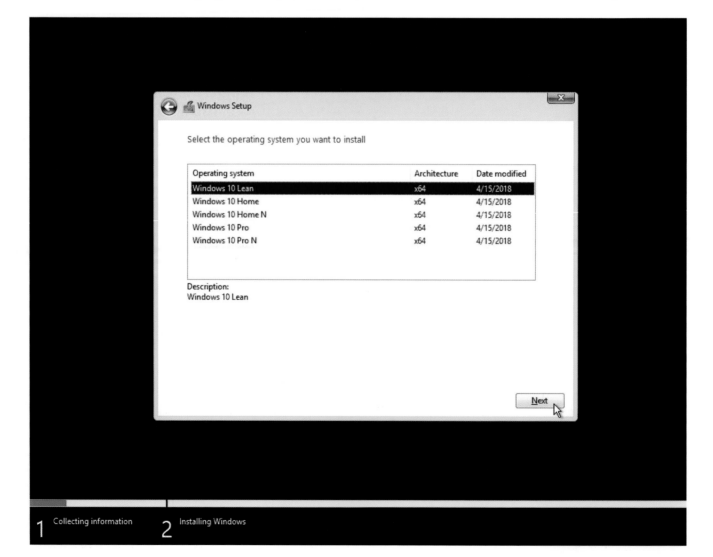

boot disc and prompt you with the following sentence: 'Press any key to boot from CD or DVD/external device...'

We'll ignore the classic joke about finding the 'any' key; simply press any button on the keyboard and the installation process will begin. You'll need to wait for a little while for the necessary files to be installed. These aren't actually the core operating system files but, instead, the tools to allow for the complete process to be done; the BIOS needs to have something available before it can begin any kind of installation process, after all.

Follow the installation process

From this point on there isn't much more we can tell you. Once Windows is ready to install you'll be greeted with what is known as an installation wizard – or a traditional mouse and keyboard system of steps to help the process along. Regardless of the version of Windows you've chosen you'll be met with a selection of language, date and time and keyboard formats – that's how you know you're ready to properly begin the installation. Though you can change these and any of the following steps once Windows has been installed, it is obviously much more beneficial to pick the choices more relevant to you throughout this process. Simply follow each of these steps and, before too long, you'll be greeted with the desktop of your gaming PC!

Windows is tied to a personal account, which you might not like. Unfortunately it's not a process that can be skipped.

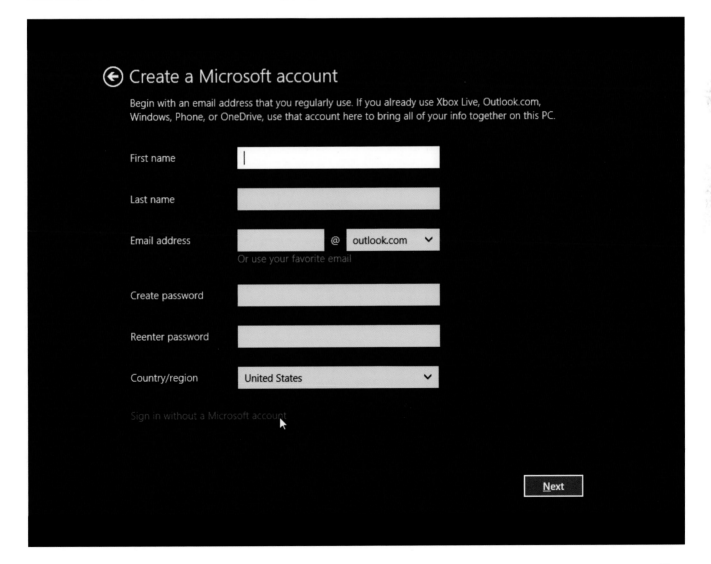

PART  What software?

So you've put the PC hardware together, you've installed your operating system and now you're looking at your computer's desktop screen. You're done! At this point, providing fire isn't bursting from your fans (honestly, that's not a possibility!) then you're free to do whatever you wish with your computer. If you really want, you can rush off and get some games installed, and test out your build for its graphical capabilities. Every gamer wants to first ogle those polygons, but hold your horses! That is certainly something you could do, but there might be some more setup left to do – in particular, you need to think about some of the important (and not-so-important) software that you want to install first.

When it comes to deciding on what software you want to get, it's important to first think about the things that are imperative not only for your gaming, but also for your computer's everyday use: this may be a gaming PC, but that likely won't be its only purpose. So think online security, think about how you plan to get your games, and think about the general everyday tools you might be needing. As with the hardware itself, it comes down to thinking about your needs first, and getting everything

in place. You could favour a method in which you download the things you need as and when you need them rather than trying to think about what you may need in the future. That's one way of doing it, sure, but to avoid clutter on your storage drives, it's a good idea to get to a foundational state that you're happy with. This way you can wipe the Downloads folder of all those unnecessary install tools (and get into the habit of clearing that folder up from time to time) as well as disable the

Always be sure to download software either from an official website or via trusted software distribution sites like Download.com

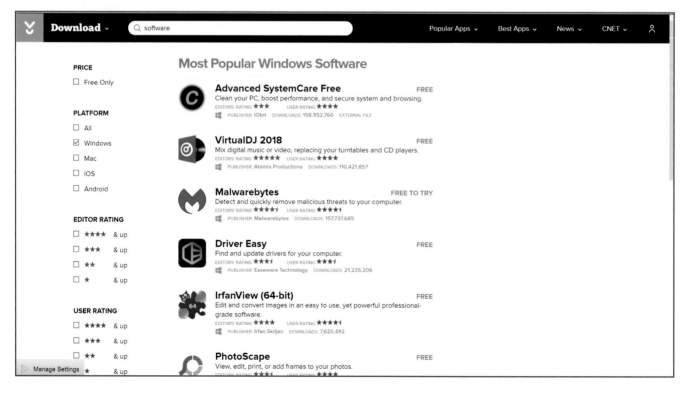

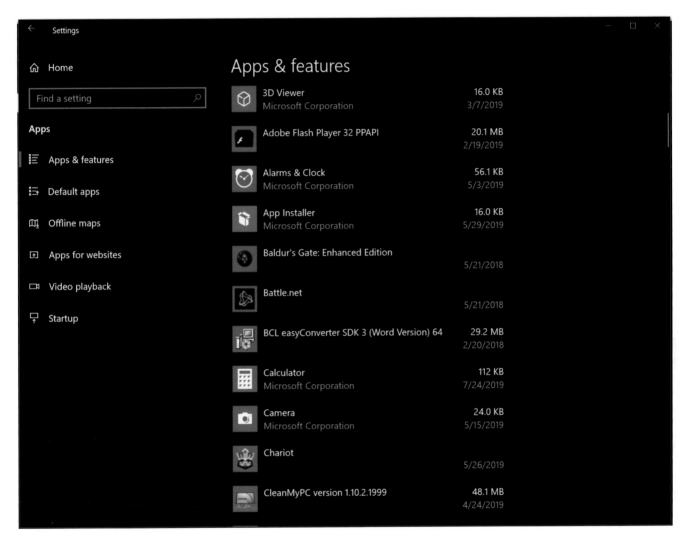

Apps & features

3D Viewer Microsoft Corporation	16.0 KB 3/7/2019	
Adobe Flash Player 32 PPAPI	20.1 MB 2/19/2019	
Alarms & Clock Microsoft Corporation	56.1 KB 5/3/2019	
App Installer Microsoft Corporation	16.0 KB 5/29/2019	
Baldur's Gate: Enhanced Edition	5/21/2018	
Battle.net	5/21/2018	
BCL easyConverter SDK 3 (Word Version) 64	29.2 MB 2/20/2018	
Calculator Microsoft Corporation	112 KB 7/24/2019	
Camera Microsoft Corporation	24.0 KB 5/15/2019	
Chariot	5/26/2019	
CleanMyPC version 1.10.2.1999	48.1 MB 4/24/2019	

software that has decided it will launch itself alongside each new start-up of your computer. But on top of that, it's a nice idea to create what's known as a 'system restore point', a sort of backup that allows you to return to a record of your computer when it was free of junk data and applications. It's handy to have should your PC fall victim to a particularly nasty virus, too.

There's no ignoring the fact that there is a sheer wealth of software out there available for you to download, and we can't by any means be a complete resource of them all. We've categorised a number of crucial programs you'll want to track down, but make sure that when it comes to downloading them, do so from the official page or a trustworthy and reliable source, like CNET.

While we're talking about all this, however, it's worth mentioning the importance of tidiness. You'll be surprised how common it is for PC users to install something for a one time use and forget all about it – at best taking up a chunk of your hard drive space, at worst slowing your PC down by taking up CPU processing with behind-the-scenes tasks. Some tools will boot up alongside your PC's start-up, too, and while this is sometimes unavoidable – most gaming keyboards and mice come with bespoke software, for example – an overload of start-up software can put an early task on your CPU that will slow it down for that session. Be vigilant about how much you install, what you do choose to install and – if you know you won't use a piece of software again, or for a while – don't be afraid to uninstall it to keep your PC feeling fresh. A tidy hard drive is an efficient hard drive.

Don't be afraid to regularly visit the Apps & features section of the Settings to remove any unwanted software.

PART  Picking a browser

The first thing you'll likely want to install onto your PC is a browser. Now, if you've installed Windows, then the chances are you've already got one installed: Internet Explorer. This is sufficient for getting the job done, but in truth there are so many more options available that it has, depending on who you're talking to, become rather redundant. By all means give it a trial run, but if you ever fancy trying out something else then there's a great number of options out there. For some, Internet Explorer – or its Windows 10 pre-installed equivalent, Microsoft Edge – has little other use than to open only once to search for (and download) a better alternative.

Internet Explorer will come pre-installed with Windows and can't be fully removed. Don't be afraid to use it to find a better browser.

But what alternative should you go for? Well, that's a tough question and, as with everything here, it'll come down to preferences and needs. Though there are many more out there, the usage market is largely shared between roughly five key competitors, and a large portion of that is thanks to particular operating systems coming with these browsers pre-installed onto their computers; some people don't even realise there are better choices out there. If we're to overlook Microsoft's offerings, then you're left with Google Chrome, Mozilla Firefox and Opera.

Google has naturally been able to eke out a lofty position at the top thanks to its dominance of the search engine market; its browser is quick, filled with extensions to customise the experience and comes with handy features like a built-in Google Translate tool and PDF viewer. Firefox is the other big name in the browser game, providing a similar level

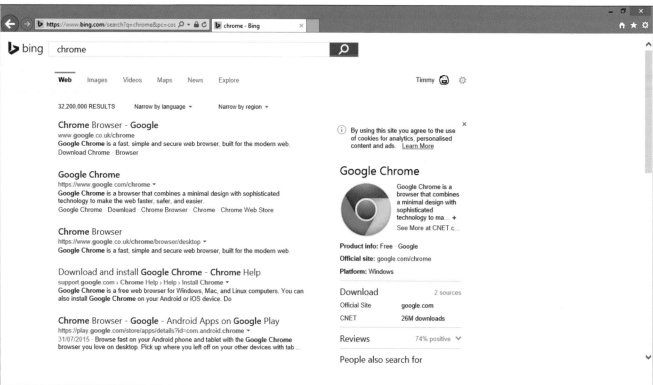

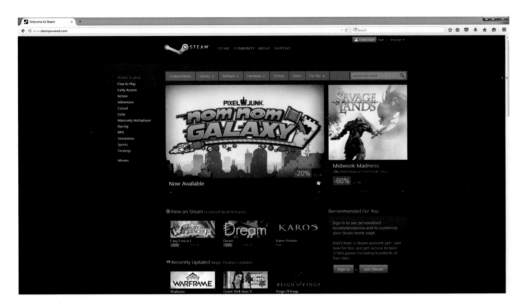

Firefox is well known for its number of additional extras you can download and install onto the browser.

of extensibility as Chrome but with greater emphasis on privacy (Google is an ads-driven company, after all, so your data is valuable to them). Then there's Opera, which is built on the same engine as Chrome – it even works with many extensions from the Chrome Web Store – and comes with a handful of really beneficial features: a built-in VPN, connectivity with instant messaging platforms and an ad blocker are all helping to make Opera one of the better choices when it comes to choice of internet browser.

Opera is still low on the market share scales, but it's a great – and quick – browser that you should at least try.

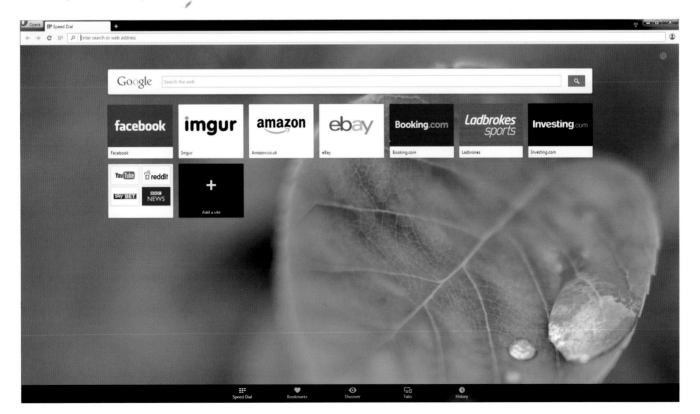

PART  Antivirus and security

With the browser out of the way you can then look to perhaps the most important piece of software you could ever download: antivirus. Sad as it is to say, but Windows PCs often find themselves victims of computer viruses and malware, digital pieces of code or software that look to sneak onto your PC, infect it and cause all sorts of trouble – ranging from CPU or memory issues to wiping important system information stored on your hard drive. It's an easily avoidable problem, however, and so long as you maintain up-to-date antivirus and firewall software and avoid visiting suspicious websites or downloading potentially harmful files then you likely won't ever get struck by such a devastating attack. Just keep an eye out for important changes in the antivirus world; thankfully decent software will automatically alert you to any concerns.

And as with all of the most important software you can download, there are myriad options available. It can be overwhelming, in fact, especially for antivirus software. It seems these days there are as many antivirus programs as there are viruses. The big names like Norton, AVG or Avast are the more popular consumer versions, but then there are the likes of McAfee, Trend or Bitdefender who might not maintain as wide a portion of the market but offer incredible – and perhaps even better – defence against a range of potential threats. While these do come with varying costs that you might want to consider for the purest protection, there are free

Good antivirus software keeps itself up to date without ever interrupting your PC usage until something is detected.

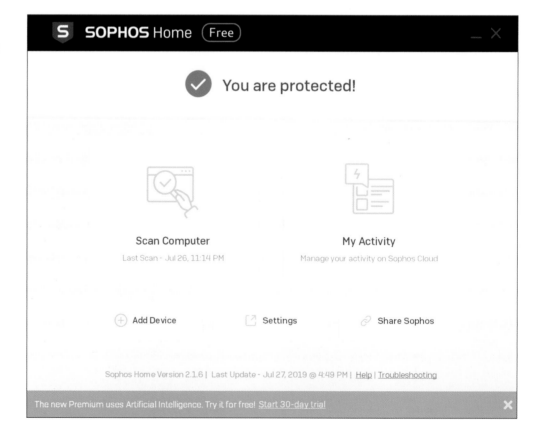

Basic

AVG AntiVirus FREE

Essential free protection
that won't let you down

- ✔ Stop viruses, spyware, & other malware
- ✔ Block unsafe links, downloads, & email attachments
- ✔ Scan for PC performance problems
- ✔ Get real time-security updates

FREE Download

Full

AVG Internet Security
Unlimited

Our UNLIMITED and best all-round
protection, whatever you do online

- ✔ Stop viruses, spyware, & other malware
- ✔ Block unsafe links, downloads, & email attachments
- ✔ Scan for PC performance problems
- ✔ Get real-time security updates
- ✔ Keep hackers away with Enhanced Firewall
- ✔ Securely shop & bank online
- ✔ Avoid fake websites for safer payments
- ✔ Block spam, scams, & phishing emails
- ✔ Phone & chat agents are on hand 24/7
- ✔ Includes unlimited AntiVirus PRO for Android™
- ✔ Installs on UNLIMITED computers

Buy Now
~~$79.99~~ $63.99

Here's what you can hope to get from free packages when compared to premium ones.

packages that offer limited but valuable security against online threats. When it comes to this stuff, even the bare minimum will be helpful.

Elsewhere, tools like password managers can be helpful additions to your suite of installed software. These will automatically store your account and password details in an encrypted vault and will automatically enter them into the login pages of websites. This is useful for protecting yourself against phishing attempts – where a fake version of an official-looking website will trick you into giving away your credentials – but more than anything it makes your life easier when it comes to general internet use.

Last is a VPN, and while this might seem like an unnecessary, paranoid extreme there are certainly benefits to making use of an encrypted internet connection, especially if – like many of us – you're becoming increasingly concerned about how your online data is being used. As with antivirus software, there are countless VPN providers to choose from, though there is an added bonus of being able to subscribe to a complete internet security suite that will provide everything you could need to keep you safe from potential threats. It's worth adding that a VPN will have a noticeable effect on your internet connection, though, so if you do fancy the enhanced security that comes from a VPN then you'll most likely want to deactivate it when playing games online if your unencrypted connection is pretty slow to begin with.

PART  Drivers and GPU software

If you're new to the world of PC gaming hardware and haven't done much tinkering around with any computer in your life, then it's important to know about device drivers. These are pieces of software that are installed into your operating system to make sure that a particular piece of hardware is compatible with the OS and will function as it's supposed to. They're the crucial tools that convert the computer's binary code of 1s and 0s into the corresponding output; for example, a device driver will ensure that your graphics card can properly pump out 3D visuals for gaming purposes. While the operating system will have a vast number of these pre-installed to assist with everyday use – think drivers for printers, mice and keyboards, the things that non-specialist users might need a PC for – when it comes to gaming hardware there are often very few cases where the OS will automatically detect and be able to operate an installed piece of hardware.

That's why one of the first things to do when setting up your PC is to download and install drivers for each of your hardware parts. In the case of your graphics card, in fact, you may even need to use the motherboard's in-built display output with your monitor temporarily, just so that your GPU can even detect a video signal. In many cases you will be provided with discs of the drivers available within the packaging, but these most certainly won't be the most up-to-date versions. It's always better to head directly to the hardware manufacturer's website and look for your hardware model to find the corresponding driver downloads. Start with your motherboard (there may be individual drivers for the chipset, audio, USB connections, etc.) and

Hardware manufacturers will always provide the latest drivers for a wide range of makes and models on their websites.

then install the GPU drivers. After that, install the drivers for peripherals like your mouse, keyboard or webcam if you're using one and lastly any specialist hardware like a microphone for streaming, a gaming headset or a graphics tablet.

One last point to remember about device drivers is that if you're having any issues with a particular hardware, step number one should be to download the latest drivers. Typically you shouldn't have any issues with your computer from one day to the next, so if you find a newly released game isn't working, then updating your GPU driver will likely resolve that issue.

On that note, there is software available from both AMD and NVIDIA that can be installed onto your computer to help with the smooth running of your graphics card. Both GeForce Experience (NVIDIA) and Radeon Software (AMD) provide the automatic updating of drivers as and when they're released, which can be beneficial for keeping your system running smoothly if you're into playing the latest video game releases. But on top of that, they each come with a selection of settings to tinker with your GPU, in-built overclocking functionality, gameplay video capture and can even detect performance during a game to suggest changes that can be made to improve optimisation of the settings. Many gamers will swear against installing what they call bloatware, but there's no harm in installing these free tools to see if they might benefit you.

PART 4

Streaming and video capture

If you're getting into building a gaming PC because you've seen the fun that people can have on Twitch or YouTube as the community of gamers join in with you while you play, then there are some important facets of your hardware and software that you should consider. While not entirely necessary, you'll want to consider some important, additional equipment alongside your computer, while having the right software to stream or record your gameplay footage and audio.

Firstly, if you want to take video content seriously then you'll need to consider a good quality microphone. Most fans of video gameplay won't care about 'raw' footage of you navigating a level, puzzle or menu; you'll need to spice it up with commentary and the only worthwhile way of doing that is with a decent quality microphone. This could be included as part of a gaming headset or a separate tabletop standing mic, but it's important all the same. This could also be said about a webcam, though in truth it's not 100% necessary to show your face, though standard practice generally means that the more recognisable streamers tend to have a picture-in-picture of themselves playing the game. Lastly, if you really want to go the whole hog, then a second monitor could be a decent idea. This way you'll have a separate screen on which you can have a browser open of your viewers' comments, and that'll be a huge boon in interacting and growing your community of fans.

When it comes to software there are a large number of options available that people will recommend, such as XSplit and Streamlabs. However, the one that comes up the most and is by far the most effective and feature-packed is OBS, Open Broadcaster Software. This suite of streaming and video recording tools is open-source software, meaning it's free for anyone to download and use. But that's not why it's so useful; its community of developers has created one of the most robust and complete streaming packages around and though it can be a bit finicky to set up at first, it's all you'll ever need to get your gameplay, camera feed and audio online at once.

Setting up a livestream is not a simple task, but OBS helps make the process that bit easier.

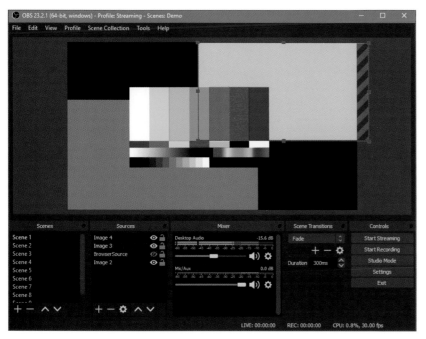

PART 4

THE FIRST START-UP
Digital distribution

You may already have noticed how PC games have been taking increasingly smaller parts of many retail outlets over the years, with some even getting rid of them entirely. The reasons for this – while numerous – are primarily down to the cultural importance of digital distribution, or a means by which you buy and own licences to your games but have no physical copy with which to store and install from. Over the years digital distribution has grown and grown to a point where it is now more common to purchase a PC game digitally than to head into a store, pick up a copy and install it onto your computer. As a result, you're going to want to know what your options are when buying a game online.

The big name in this regard is Steam, the incredibly popular service and program that the majority of gamers use to buy, download and access their PC games. It's handy for keeping everything in one place, has regular sales and wish list functionalities to ensure you're not paying over the odds, while a bevy of social and technical features help to keep gamers connected and in control. It's essentially

mandatory for PC gaming, these days. Taking Steam as an example, these applications are typically loaded up initially before accessing any given game, acting as a sort of modern-day DRM (digital rights management) due to the requirement of an internet connection and a user account to access the games within the service. It's a necessary evil for developers and publishers to combat piracy – which had been

Steam is by no means the only digital distribution platform these days, but it's certainly the main one.

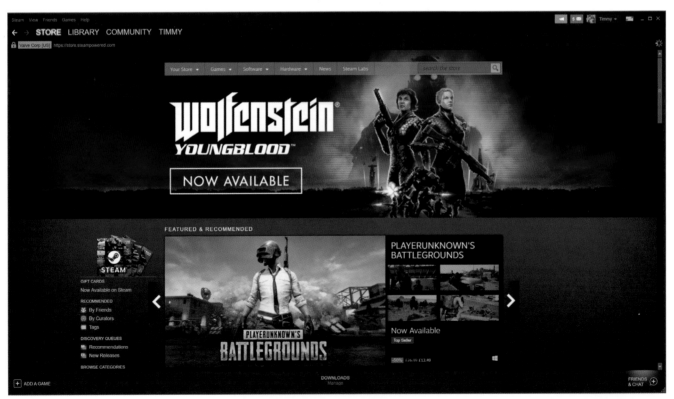

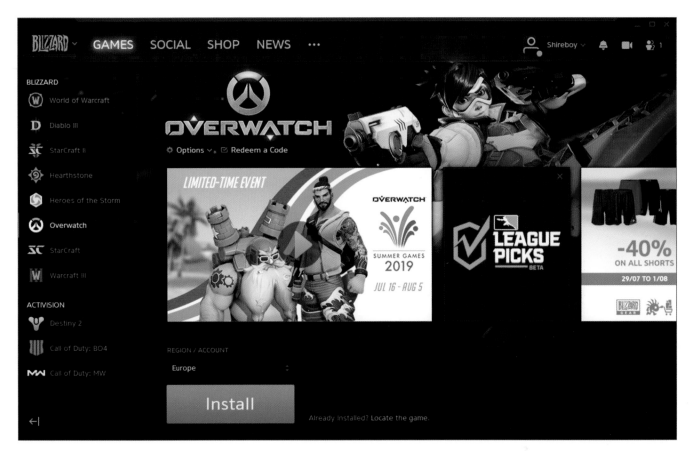

a significant problem in the years prior to such platforms – but has become a minor extra step that most are willing to endure these days. Since you'll almost never get a modern game on an install disc these days, it's not something any of us can really begin to question anyway.

A large reason for digital distribution's popularity lies in the benefits it offers for everyone involved. Gamers can get immediate access to their library without the need for swapping discs, with only a need to wait for a download to finalise. In most cases updates can be automatically downloaded, too, meaning that any issues that the developer has sought to fix – or even new content that has been added to the game – is ready for you the moment it's needed.

Once upon a time, Steam was the only place gamers could go for their games, and for a long while it seemed like it was enough. Other big-name publishers have been moving into their own digital distribution platforms these days though, with Electronic Arts' games available exclusively through Origin or Ubisoft providing its own store alongside its social service UPlay. Then there's GOG.com, which used to focus on

getting old games to run on modern computers but these days specialises in selling indie games and hidden gems. The most recent addition is the Epic Games Store, however, which has been making aggressive attempts to cut into Steam's domination of the PC gaming industry by providing creators with greater percentages of the sales and some games even releasing exclusively on the platform. Not everyone is keen on this move, in part because Steam has been the de facto PC gaming platform for so long now that any attempt to split up a gamer's vast library of games is seen as a threat to a simpler, more efficient way of life. That's true, if Epic Games Store really is able to solidify its place in the market, then you will need to switch between at least two different platforms to play and get the best value on the games that you want, but this extra competition can only be good for consumers in the long run.

On top of these, there are other services online that will sell codes to use on digital distribution platforms – such as through Amazon – while a couple of other services, such as GreenManGaming, do offer their own

Many big-name developers and publishers will have their own launchers where their games are automatically kept up to date.

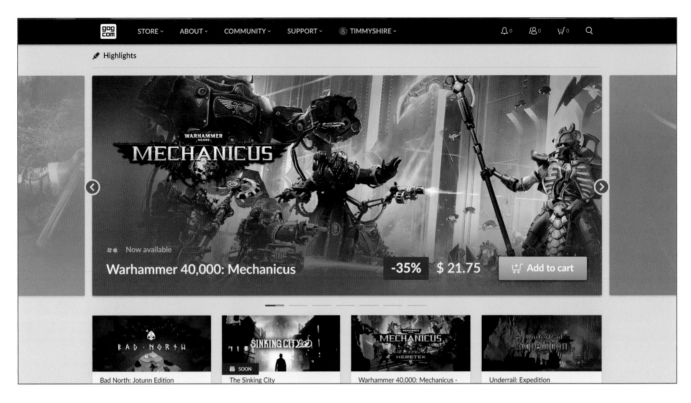

Some digital distribution platforms, like GOG.com, specialise in the types of games they sell rather than trying to compete with Steam.

Metro Exodus is one of the best games for testing the graphical prowess of your machine, but it caused controversy when it was released due to its exclusivity to the Epic Games Store.

downloadable program, too. Don't forget that there are some games that will first require a patcher to be loaded before you can actually access the game, since many always-online multiplayer titles require every player to be running the same version to properly access the server. Developers like Blizzard have their own launcher that, much like the mentioned

platforms above, will automatically update your games before you access them.

Unfortunately, there's no avoiding these platforms, but aside from the likes of Steam and perhaps the Epic Games Store, there's no need to rush out and download the programs straight away. It's enough to work on a case-by-case basis.

PART 4 Storage cleaning

While not directly tied to gaming itself, there's no denying that keeping your storage drive clean and optimised is a great way to keep your system running smoothly and effectively. Over the years, your computer's storage can become crammed with unwanted, unnecessary or even unused data. The more data on your hard disk or SSD, the more there is to check and clarify at any one time. It's not something you may notice happening, but eventually an overclogged storage drive can have an impact on your computer's performance – especially if you're running low on space. The problem is, manually rifling through all your folders and files periodically isn't fun, and nor is it effective since you'll almost always miss something.

Keep on top of the junk data on your PC and it'll go a long way to keeping your system running smoothly.

As such, it might be worthwhile to consider installing software to do this for you. There are countless programs available that can scour your disk drives to find out what is worthless and can be removed. Many of them come with built-in tools to help in numerous other manners too, such as defragmentation or application removal, essentially making these suites more about general system optimisation rather than purely cleaning up your disk drives. Picking one from the many available packages can be tricky, especially since you'll need to think about whether you want a free option, a per-licence payment or the choice of a subscription for regular updates to the software. The name CCleaner has remained a staple in the industry for years and provides most of the core features for free, so if you're stuck with figuring out what your own personal needs are on this front then this is a safe option to go for.

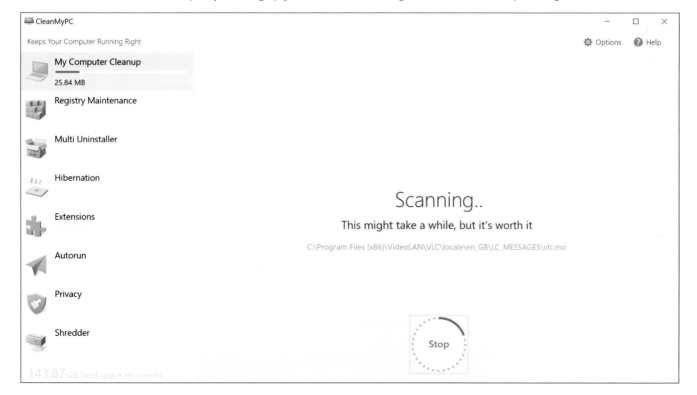

PART

Social software, and the rest...

What use is your super-powered gaming PC if you can't share it with anyone? Multiplayer gaming has risen to become a significant aspect of the industry, with even most single-player, story-focused games coming with a competitive or cooperative online option too. And sure, while the majority of these modes can be played solo, joining in with a random selection of players through various matchmaking services, there's no denying that the thrill of playing with people you actually know is all the more rewarding – win or lose. Even more besides, whether you want to play with your friends or not, having a means to talk and share your gaming experiences with other people will be imperative to making the most of your PC.

Once upon a time this was achieved through specialised software like Raptr or XFire, but with the common practice of most friends circles connecting via WhatsApp or Messenger groups on their smartphones, these services ultimately died out. It's still possible to keep in touch via in-built instant messaging tools that can be found in many clients for gaming, but unless you also want to make the switch to a smartphone app you'll need to be both online and actively playing on the same platforms as your friends to get in touch with them.

That's not to say that there aren't plenty of extra options on top of the in-built, closed nature of many other games and platforms, however. But there are numerous other tools, apps and services that could be very useful at some point. To help with that, we've created a final table to collate all of the important social and non-social software to help you get a better grasp of the things you should look for and download, or as a reference to return to should you find you suddenly have a need for such programs. Many of these you won't need right away, others you will, but in either case it's worth knowing about their existence should the need arise.

Mixing football and acrobatic, rocket-powered remote control cars might not seem like an obvious combination, but *Rocket League* is easily one of the most exciting multiplayer games available at the moment. The small teams means it's easy for friends to get together, too.

Software	Use for...	Details
Discord	Connecting with your friends.	Discord has grown over the years to become a place where many gaming communities – whether custom-created or those passionate about the same games and topics as you – choose to hang out or make plans. Perfect for instant messaging or voice calls.
Dropbox	Sharing files.	There are multiple cloud storage options, but if you find yourself commonly sharing files then a shared Dropbox among friends will be very useful.
7-Zip	Extracting and compiling groups of files.	7-Zip features the widest range of compatible compile-file types, so it's likely if you come across anything other than a .zip file you'll have use for this. The .7z can only be opened by this software.
WinRAR	Extracting and compiling groups of files.	The alternative option for extracting and compiling files, WinRAR is always active and doesn't require you to open a separate program to use it. Though its range of compatible files is wide, there are some it cannot handle.
Razer Cortex	PC settings optimisation.	By working with any type of gaming platform, Razer Cortex is a handy tool for detecting and enhancing your gaming experience with minimal effort on your part.
VLC	Video playback.	There are a wide number of video file types, and even among the most popular a number of different codecs to run them; VLC will run them all with its very lightweight, simple software.
KeePass	Password management.	To ensure that all your online accounts are secure, consider downloading KeePass to keep your passwords safe, secure and easily referenced. Allows you to use multiple different passwords without having to memorise them all.
Skype	Connecting and speaking with friends.	Skype is not a svelte piece of software and can take up a lot of memory and CPU resources, but has instant message features, is widely used outside of gaming and can be useful for smaller groups of friends.
TeamSpeak	Speaking with a group of friends.	Allows a huge number of users (512 on non-commercial, non-profit servers) that can each be arranged by groups. Very specialised, but just as useful among smaller groups.
Mumble	Speaking with a group of friends.	Open-source software so is completely free to download and use. It is particularly lightweight with high-quality audio, making it one of the more popular voice chat options.
LogMeIn	Virtual LAN creation.	By being able to create a VPN connection through LogMeIn, you'll be able to safely, securely and privately create a game server for you and your friends to play on.
Nexus Mod Manager	Modding management tool.	If you get into modding your PC games for different experiences, then making use of the Nexus Mod Manager (NexusMods is sort of an online resource for all things modding) will make the process much easier to handle.
OBS	Streaming your gameplay.	Livestreaming has become a big factor of PC gaming, and OBS is a free piece of software that is both lightweight and feature rich. One of the best options for streaming your gameplay onto places like Twitch.tv and YouTube.
Utorrent	Download BitTorrent files.	Some games – particularly large online games like MMOs – allow the option to download official game files via torrent, a quicker method of data transfer.
F.lux	Night mode for your PC.	Like the similar Night Mode that many smartphones have, f.lux is a handy tool that can be set up and customised to activate when it gets dark so as to reduce the glare from your screen when gaming at night.
GIMP	Image editing.	Free PhotoShop alternative that includes many of the important features of the paid-for equivalent, including layer and layer masks.
Adobe PDF	Open and view PDF files.	There will be a time where you need to open a PDF file, whether for gaming or not. There are many alternatives, but Adobe's own PDF viewer is a fine option.
SumatraPDF	Open and view PDF files.	As an alternative to Adobe's own software, Sumatra is the most popular free equivalent. Doesn't run in the background, includes numerous options and is very quick to use.
LibreOffice	Create and edit text, spreadsheet and Powerpoint files.	While Microsoft Office is the most popular option for businesses, LibreOffice provides the same features for free. These days, there's no need to pay for an office suite of software.
HoneyView	Image viewer.	The basic image viewing software as part of Windows is fine, but HoneyView is much quicker, sleeker and is compatible with many more file types.
Foobar2k	Audio player.	If music is important to you, Windows Media Player is not software you want to use. There are plenty of free options available, but Foobar2k is the most popular these days. Quick and light software.
iTunes	Manage media files.	While we would never condone using iTunes – as a piece of software it is horrific and intrusive – sadly it's a necessity if you own an iPod, iPad or iPhone.

5

PART 5 Accessories

Razer manufactures a wide range of PC accessories – everything from mice and keyboards to headsets and gaming controllers.

When putting together the perfect gaming PC it's easy to overlook the importance of all the extras that go with it. When you're throwing half your budget into the graphics card, it's understandable that you might reconsider the amount you're willing to spend on the accessories and peripherals – and when there's as much choice as there is, it's often easier just to go for the simplest option. But remember this: while the hardware inside your PC might be core to making your gaming experience technically flawless, the accessories you use will factor in just how comfortable your gaming can be.

Take, for example, something as simple as a mouse. Sure, you can pick a cheap gaming mouse and it does the job, it moves the cursor around and that's all you need, right? But what about its DPI or in-built acceleration? What type of sensor does the mouse have and does it have the right number of additional buttons? Even the shape of it and its ergonomic design will play a huge part in how useful that mouse is for gaming. It's a surprisingly convoluted process to pick out the right tool for the job, and the same goes for keyboards and headsets and even added extras like racing wheels and joysticks. The games you enjoy playing will directly affect not only the peripherals you need to buy, but what features you need to look for from each of them.

And that's still overlooking the confusing world of monitors, which ranges from the cheap-and-cheerful HD LCD displays to the

high-end, super-fast refresh rates or the perfect colour reproduction with the likes of IPS panels. If you thought mice were overwhelming then you've yet to experience the trials that come with buying the right monitor for gaming. We've broken down each of the accessories into the key facets you'll need to consider for the optimum gaming experience, deciphered the marketing babble that comes with them and given you the necessary information to know that the choice you land on is the right one. We've even bundled in a few suggestions of our own, though don't let that be the deciding factor; when it comes to PC peripherals and gaming it's all down to what you need, and that changes from person to person. We've tried to cover every possible need for every possible type of gamer – that includes those interested in streaming gameplay – but that ultimate decision can only come down to you.

PART 5 Gaming mice

The problem with mice – especially for gamers – is that what makes the 'best' mouse is, in a lot of ways, completely subjective and really comes down to what it is you want to get from the peripheral. Every PC needs one, obviously, but if you play a lot of MMOs over shooters then the features and benefits that you're looking for from a mouse will vary quite dramatically. The shape of it, how it 'fits' in your hand and even the weight are a big deal when looking for the one that is right for you; it's important to have a think about what it is you need from a mouse before even beginning to look for one to buy. On the plus side it's not entirely mandatory that your choice has all the bells and whistles – a basic option will, for the most part, work just as well as its competition. And since the majority these days are USB-powered, plug-and-play mice, you don't need to worry quite so much about compatibility.

What to look for

DPI – This is the measurement that you're going to encounter a lot when looking at purchasing a mouse. This stands for dots per inch, less often referred to as the more technically accurate CPI, or counts per inch. The higher the DPI the 'quicker' it will read your movements, essentially meaning that you'll need to move the mouse less to get the same responses of a lower-DPI mouse. Thankfully most modern gaming mice will allow you to tweak the DPI settings, while others even feature activated precision modes

– whereby a button on the mouse will drop the DPI to get that precision, allowing you to quickly un-toggle once more.

Sensors – Ye olde trackball mice are something of an antiquity these days, with gaming mice instead using two types of sensors: optical and laser. The former uses an LED light and a sensor camera to track the movement and is better at maintaining response when lifting the mouse or using it on an uneven surface. Laser mice are more common for gaming, though, and enable

much better precision with much less jitter (or the misreading of a surface). Of the two you'll likely want to go with laser.

Acceleration – Most mice will have some form of acceleration, a feature whereby the cursor will move faster the faster you move the mouse itself. It can be beneficial in some circumstances, such as if you have a smaller mouse mat or desk space to enable smaller movements of the mouse itself. However, acceleration is generally disliked by many gamers since it means you're not getting the exact one-for-one control over the cursor and there's an element of unpredictability about cursor movement. It's unlikely it'll be too heavy-handed in gaming mice, and can usually be disabled.

Extra buttons – Every mouse will have at least two buttons, and in all likelihood a clickable scroll wheel, too. When it comes to gaming you're going to want at least a couple of extra buttons built into the mouse itself for that extra

speed and efficiency when playing. MOBAs like *League of Legends*, for example, rely on fast reactions and the quicker you can pull off that clutch manoeuvre the more of an advantage you will have. The games you play will affect how many buttons you might need – MMO players will likely want a higher number on their mouse – but it's about finding a balance between comfort and usability and the advantage extra buttons bring.

Mouse suggestions

Logitech G502 Proteus Spectrum

RRP: £79.99
If you're not looking for any specific needs and would rather have a great gaming mouse capable of doing it all, then the G502 is certainly one of the best options right now. Its 11 buttons are all programmable to give you full control of the device, it has a high 16,000 DPI sensor and even comes with five different weights for customisation of how heavy it is to lug around the mousepad.

Razer Naga Trinity

RRP: £99.99
Razer's Naga range has long been considered the go-to option for MMOs thanks to the numerous extra buttons on the side. The Trinity model takes things further, though, with interchangeable side plates to allow for either 2, 7, or 12 additional buttons, making it the most versatile mouse on the market and capable of assisting you with normal use, MOBA play or MMO gaming.

Corsair M65 RGB Elite

RRP: £49.99
If FPS games are more your thing then you'll definitely want to pick up the Corsair M65. Not only does it have a high 18,000 DPI range for great speed and accuracy but it features a toggle-able 'sniper mode', which switches to a low DPI for precision targeting – an important feature for FPS fans. It's quite a heavy mouse too, which is as much a warning as praise – FPS gamers will need that for greater control.

Razer Deathadder Elite

RRP: £69.99
Mostly what makes the Razer Deathadder Elite such a good mouse is its carefully considered design. This is by far and away one of the best gaming mice in terms of fit, and while it only has two additional buttons for a large majority of games there isn't really much more you need. It's a luxury option but certainly one of the better ones out there.

PART  Gaming keyboards

Gaming keyboards are much easier to pinpoint than mice. Where the latter needs to fit a very particular feel, the former is much more objectively measured. The primary choice is between a mechanical keyboard (so the keys are individual switches) and a membrane keyboard. There are pros and cons for both, though mechanical keyboards tend to win out in terms of reliability. Serious gamers should definitely consider a mechanical keyboard, but if you're after a cheaper, more portable option (for LANs perhaps) there are still some great membrane keyboards on the market. Outside of that there isn't really much to distinguish between many options besides their ergonomic design and the extra gadgets they might offer, such as additional, customisable keys.

What to look for

Mechanical versus Membrane – Since this will be your big decision, it's worth spending some time looking at the options. As already mentioned, mechanical keyboards use a system of separate switches so that each key you press is exactly that – there's no confusion between multiple key presses, they'll last you much longer and they feel more consistent in use. But it does take some getting used to a mechanical keyboard, they are heavier than their membrane counterparts and they are considerably more expensive. Mechanical will always be better in terms of gaming, but it might not be worth the cost.

Cherry MX – If you are looking at mechanical keyboards then you may see the term 'Cherry MX Switches' of varying colours pop up. These are references to the types of mechanical switches being used in that keyboard with red, brown and blue being the most common. Red are unrestricted, linear switches preferred for gaming – their lack of restriction makes them much more

responsive. Brown and blue offer a much more tactile response with a noticeable 'bump' to let you know a key has been pressed, with brown being a quieter key and blue still offering the louder click as you type. Your situation will affect which of these you want, though these days manufacturers are finding their own solutions to this situation.

Backlighting – It might seem like a minor thing, but backlighting is quite an important feature to have. It can come in a variety of styles – sometimes just the spaces between the keys, other times just the lettering and sometimes both – and usually the colour and brightness can be customised. It's a good feature to have, especially for LAN attenders – often the dark rooms will make it hard to see where your fingers are resting, and backlighting will fix that.

Macro/extra keys – Some keyboards bring additional buttons along with them, ranging from a handful of macro keys on the far left to a whole new array often presented like another ten-key number pad. How useful these are will depend on the games you play: MMO and perhaps RTS players will get quite a lot from these extra key binding options, but most players won't really have much use for them. When looking into this feature, try to evaluate how close those extra keys are either to the WASD or the directional buttons, since that will directly correlate to how easy they are to access mid-game.

Media keys – Perhaps less important for gaming, media keys are a set of additional buttons that directly affect any videos or music you might be playing through media software – whether that's skipping or pausing, or increasing and lowering the volume. It's a handy extra to have, admittedly, but be warned that rarely are these buttons hardwired to correspond with the operating systems themselves, meaning you'll likely need to install and run software just to set them up and use them and even then they're not always reliable.

Wrist rests – Though not entirely a necessary option to include since you can purchase gel wrist rests anyway, it's worth thinking about the comfort of the keyboard you're going to be buying. If you're spending a lot of money, you'll want to know that it can at least be used in a relaxed manner, and often a rest specialised for the keyboard itself will feel better than an optional gel equivalent. If the keyboard has a longer section (beneath the spacebar) you may not need one anyway, so try to consider the shape of keyboard you're after as well as the position it'll be placed on your desk so you know 100% that it won't cause any damage to your wrists.

Keyboard suggestions

Razer Cynosa Chroma

RRP: £64.99

This mechanical keyboard offers pretty much everything you might need from a great gaming keyboard: great design, backlighting, silent MX keys and non-intrusive software too. But it's not incredibly expensive like so many keyboards; while you could certainly opt for a membrane keyboard for less, there aren't many mechanical boards as good as this that you could get cheaper.

Corsair K70 RBG Mk.2

RRP: £169.99

Corsair's range ticks all the right boxes with Cherry MX Red switches, individual backlighting customisation for each key (so you can highlight WASD, for example) and a gripped wrist rest. Alternatives come in the FPS-focus keyboard that comes with contorted movement and weapon select keys, or the K95 – which is essentially the K70 but with a set of bindable keys and stored profiles for different games.

Logitech G Pro

RRP: £99.99

As a better option for LAN events, the Logitech G Pro is lightweight and compactly designed while still maintaining a good ergonomic look and feel. Since it is all-purpose, it's not as fancy as the higher-end models, but in terms of comfort to use when space available is at a premium, there are few that can beat this keyboard.

SteelSeries Apex Pro

RRP: £199.99

While the price tag might be off-putting, this keyboard has solidified itself as the hardcore gamer's dream. It has adjustable per-key mechanical switches in the keys, allowing you to control the sensitivity of each key individually and therefore allowing you to customise your gaming experience to your needs. An OLED screen provides info from certain games, too, adding that extra advantage.

PART 5 Monitors

Buying a monitor for gaming is even more arduous than buying a new TV; while you're looking at all the same tech details – such as contrast ratio – you now also want to pay more attention to refresh rate and response time. What this amounts to is a lot of confusing numbers and no real certainty that the one you'll get is the best; hopefully we can dispel some of those concerns. Further questions are derived from how you want your set-up to look: do you want to run multiple screens? A single larger one? A wider screen with an unusual aspect ratio? There are too many options, too many variables to consider, so we've picked out the key facets you need to know about buying the best PC gaming monitor.

What to look for

Aspect ratio – Gaming monitors come in all shapes and sizes, and aspect ratio – or the width of the screen versus the height – is a large reason for this. But as gaming dimensions have become a little more standardised over the years, 16:9 is the standard to aim for. This will be the same as your TV, most likely, and if you're not too fussy about how much of your games you can see then it's easier just to stick with this. If you want a wider viewpoint in-game, however, for a kind of vision more akin to our own human eyes then you might want to look into wider aspect ratios. Again

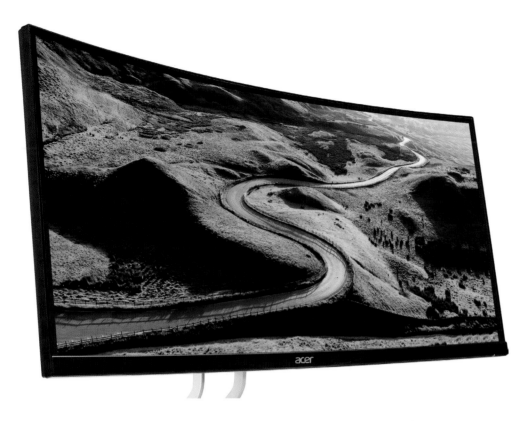

these can be in a variety of sizes, but 21:9 is the more common option, meaning more games are likely to be compatible with this size.

Resolution versus size – It's easy to say 'just go for the highest resolution', but up to a certain point an increase in resolution is actually irrelevant. At around 21 inches you're not really going to need to spend the extra to increase the resolution. If you start going over that, however, you'll probably want to start looking at higher-res screens. This will be affected by the aspect ratio you're going for too, naturally, but with bigger screens you're going to want as high a resolution as possible since it will mean not only more detail in your games but also in every aspect of your PC usage. Remember though, boosting a game's output resolution is one of the most significant impacts you'll make to your overall performance, so if you're aiming for 4K gaming then you'll need a GPU (or two) to achieve that.

Refresh rates and hertz – This is often played up as an important feature for gaming monitors and that's true, it is. However, what many overlook is the possible frame rate you're capable of producing with your games. Your potential frame rate is affected by the graphics card you have installed; if you are only capable of producing 30 frames a second, then it doesn't matter how fast your refresh rate is, it

will still be limited by that. If you're capable of 60 or more, however, then you're going to want as fast a refresh rate as possible. 60Hz (or hertz) is the standard for most gaming monitors, but it's not uncommon for 120Hz, 144Hz or 240Hz to be built into modern monitors. If your PC is going to be a beast, then you want as high a refresh rate as possible – it'll produce a smoother image, look much nicer during play and will be much more relaxing for your eyes.

Response time – Your monitor's response time is essentially the speed at which it is capable of updating with a new input or image. This is measured in milliseconds, so the lower the better. Most monitors will have a response time of roughly 8ms or less, but the better gaming monitors will measure either 2ms or 5ms. Try not to go for anything worse than 16ms, however, since that's when you'll start noticing a difference.

Type of panels – One last thing to consider is the type of panel you're choosing to use, with choices between the standard TN panels or the newer technology of IPS panels. TN panels are more common and generally offer good brightness and low power consumption, but cheaper monitors can have poor colour accuracy, especially at non-perfect viewing angles. IPS monitors are much better in this regard with practically perfect image clarity at very high viewing angles with great colour reproduction. Sadly they are considerably more expensive as a result, use a lot more power and don't feature the higher refresh rates of TN panels. It's a balancing act, then, but if you're not sparing any expense then an IPS monitor might be the one to go for.

Monitor suggestions

Asus ROG Swift

RRP: £619.99
It might be expensive, but it features an incredible response time, toggleable refresh rates, NVIDIA's G-Sync technology built in and is even 3D ready. Simply put, it is the best WQHD (Wide Quad HD) monitor out there and if you can afford the expense, it's well worth considering. It might not be a 4K monitor, but at 2560x1440 resolution it's not to be sneezed at.

Acer Predator X27

RRP: £1,499.99
While this monitor doesn't have quite the same amount of tech as the Asus ROG Swift, it does have a native 4K screen with the same built-in G-Sync technology. It's by no means affordable,

but since it is capable of 4K resolutions, which means it is a monitor that you'll want to pair up with a pretty powerful rig, otherwise you may find it not quite able to reach all of those pixels – leaving it looking a little fuzzy.

Acer XR382CQK

RRP: £899.99
If you want a widescreen monitor then Acer has the one for you. At a resolution of 3840x1600 it is one of the highest-resolution widescreen monitors available, while its IPS panel means you'll get perfect clarity. The 24:10 aspect ratio is wider than any other and so isn't totally familiar with PC gaming just yet, but you'll be glad to try it out for the first time on this screen.

BenQ EL2870U

RRP: £259
4K doesn't need to be prohibitively expensive, and that's the case with this BenQ screen. But more than that, like its predecessors it also sports a 1ms response time, an insanely high contrast ratio meaning deeper blacks and whiter whites, and even built-in speakers (though you'll likely still want to use a headset for the best sound quality). Recommended for the budget conscious.

PART **5**

Headsets and microphones

To get the best audio from your PC gaming it might seem counter-intuitive to use a headset, but the personal audio space is a much more immersive experience than even the best PC-compatible stereo systems. Buying a headset isn't quite as littered with jargon as most other accessories, but there are some features you'll want to keep an eye out for. As ever it's about asking the right questions. Do you want the most detailed sound quality? Do you want the clearest microphone and chat options? Are you planning on streaming? It's a minefield of options, but the first step is to know what you're after.

What to look for

Ear covering – There are two types of headsets, over-ear and on-ear. The difference might not sound too great, but it basically affects how insulated your sound is. Over-ear headsets have much thicker padding that cover the entirety of the ear; this produces a noise-cancelling effect

that means external sounds will be blocked out with varying model-dependent levels of success. While this gives you much better sound while playing, often these headsets can 'pinch' a little – and some users might feel discomfort over extended periods of play, especially with cheaper models. On-ear, conversely, are much lighter and generally sit – as the name suggests – on your ear. External sounds will disrupt your in-game audio, naturally, but the lighter build and fit of these types generally make them more comfortable for longer play.

Microphone types – The quality of any given microphone is dependent on the make and model you're going for, and as always the more you pay the more likely this particular feature will be improved. Noise-cancellation is something you're going to want to look for in a headset microphone, and most will advertise this when it is included. It simply means the microphone will more likely pick up just your voice, rather than other external sounds such as game audio or other people in the same room as you. For a headset, look for a directional microphone, i.e. one that points at your mouth. However, streamers are known for using a desktop boom mic to free their head of the unwieldy peripheral.

Surround sound – Like with any speaker system, looking for Dolby's surround-sound options is a sure-fire way of spotting a good-quality audio option. This does translate into greater expense, obviously, but when it comes to gaming the added benefit of surround-sound audio can be an important addition. Consider a game like *Call of Duty* or *Battlefield*: being able to detect where an enemy is by listening to the sound of their footsteps or gunfire gives you a much more intuitive, natural advantage that they might not have. So surround sound isn't just about the quality of the audio but the fact that it gives you a step-up in-game. Dolby 7.1 is the best you'll get, but 5.1 and less is viable if you prefer cheaper options.

In-line controls – It seems like such a mundane thing to mention, especially when a large number of headsets all come with controls built into the cable itself. But it's important since these will usually let you alter the volume of both game audio and voice chat via the controls, as well as mute your own microphone. They can come with varying options, so if possible try and take a look at the in-line controls available on any potential purchase so you know your needs are accounted for here.

Frequency response range – Now this might sound like jargon, and to some extent it is, but these days with modern headsets it's largely irrelevant and many don't even bother to advertise the possible range. The frequency response range of any audio device is the measurement of its lowest bass and highest treble, and while the wider the range the better, there is obviously a limit to how much we as humans can hear anyway. Practically every headset these days offers the same range of 20–20,000Hz.

Headset and microphone suggestions

HyperX Cloud

RRP: £99.99
HyperX has a solid name for producing high quality products, and its headsets are no different. The Cloud range have numerous different models and types, so sorting through even just this selection can be a challenge. However, the Cloud Alpha is a well-rounded set with a great frequency response of 13–27,000Hz, and all the necessary features that are so crucial to a great audio experience.

SteelSeries Arctis

RRP: £179.99
The SteelSeries Arctis range are great ones to pick if you're looking to splash out a bit more for the audio of your computer, in particular the Pro for the complete package – even with tasteful LED lighting for the ultimate geek chic – though the 9X is a great choice if you hope to use this audio device on other platforms, too.

Turtle Beach Elite Pro 2

RRP: £149.99
When it comes to gaming headsets, Turtle Beach has long been the name to beat. The Elite Pro range are its high-end models, and offer some of the best sound reproduction on the market. There's a few neat little extras

bundled in there too, which might sound like marketing speak but do actually help with the quality of the sound. It's comfortable to wear, too, which is a surprisingly rare advantage.

Blue Yeti Microphone

RRP: £129.99
Widely considered by countless YouTubers and streamers to be the microphone of choice when it comes to recording – or uploading – your own voice audio. Whether it's for podcasts, video narration or directly with gameplay via Twitch, Blue's Yeti microphone has secured itself as the number one for a reason. It's not a necessary purchase right away – a decent headset microphone will do – but if you take streaming seriously then this will be yours eventually.

Gaming controllers

With the rising popularity of games consoles it has become increasingly common for their PC equivalents to come with built-in controller functions, often making these games better to play if you discard the keyboard and mouse entirely. Moreover, many recent games – in particular 2D indie games – are often much better when played with a pad in your hand than the claw-shaped hunch you might have traditionally. That might sound incredulous to some hard-core PC gamers, but the truth is that in this day and age having a good-quality gaming controller to hand is imperative for most PC gamers.

What to look for

Games console design – Too often manufacturers try to add to the tried-and-tested official console designs, but for no reason. Look for something that tries to keep the simplicity of a console controller (otherwise you're better just sticking with a keyboard), with four face buttons, two analogue sticks, a D-Pad and trigger buttons too. Anything else is an optional – and arguably unnecessary – extra.

Heavyweight pads – The thing about controllers is, unlike a mouse and keyboard, you're actually holding on to them. It might seem like an odd thing to suggest, but looking for a heavier controller could actually lead to a more comfortable experience; often lightweight controllers have cheaper quality builds, and a heavier weight just feels more compelling to use. That doesn't mean it should be heavy, of course, your hands won't want to take a break.

Wired versus wireless – It's a question you might have asked about keyboards and mice, too, but here it's more of a matter of personal taste. A wired controller will give you a much simpler set-up process, while a wireless one obviously gives you greater freedom of movement when playing – even if it does require new batteries or recharging from time to time.

Controller suggestions

Microsoft Xbox 360 controller for PC

RRP: £29.99
This is the very same controller that was so well loved for the Xbox 360 but with a wire. As a Microsoft product, its drivers are built into Windows so in most cases it should be as simple as plugging it into a USB port and playing, without any real struggle. If you already have a wireless Xbox 360 or Xbox One controller, you can even buy a USB adapter and use that.

Razer Wolverine Tournament Edition Chroma

RRP: £119.99
It's much more expensive for what is, essentially, another Xbox One controller, but Razer brings a PC mindset to this pad. It's got four sensibly placed, customisable buttons – if that's something you need – an improved D-Pad, customisable lighting on the buttons and a unique 'Hair Trigger' mode that allows for quicker firing in FPS games. It's the option to go for if you really care about a gaming controller.

Sony DualShock 4

RRP: £49.99
PlayStation and Xbox have always had a rivalry and nowhere is that more apparent than with their controllers, with devout users on either side. It's a case of picking your poison, really, but the overall build quality of the DualShock 4 edges it out, even if you will need to download some software to get it to function with your PC. There's not much point getting the Xbox One equivalent if you can pick up a 360 one for less.

Logitech Gamepad F310

RRP: £24.99
If you want to avoid using a controller as much as possible and only want a budget option for when you simply have to use a gamepad, then this will be the one for you. It uses the familiar parallel analogue stick design of the DualShock and is very easy to set up, but it is cheaper and feels it too. A great option to chuck in for the LAN events, however.

ACCESSORIES

Racing wheels

If racing games are your thing – and there is a great range of simulation racers only on PC – then you really ought to consider the extra expense of a racing wheel, offering an unbeatable experience when monitoring apexes and finding racing lines. You'll need the extra space on your desk to compensate for the size of these things, but if that's not an issue and you're keen to make the most of your virtual driving experience then considering this added extra will add a whole new layer of enjoyment to your racing games.

What to look for

Force feedback – It might not sound like much, but the addition of vibration in a racing wheel is enough to separate a great wheel from an average one. Much like the way console controllers use the vibration to provide extra sensory information for a game, its inclusion in a racing wheel is what helps you distinguish the right points to brake, accelerate and even turn corners. This is a key feature.

Pedals and gearstick – Not every racing wheel will come with a set of pedals and a gearstick, and that might be better for you – the two will take up more room and there is always

compensation in the form of on-wheel buttons. But for that true racing experience, for that real sensation that you're in the driver's seat, you should consider at least a set of pedals too.

Rotation angle – This might be low down on the list of important features, but for the authentic experience you're looking for as high a rotation angle as you can possibly get. Many racing wheels lock at a certain angle and while the game will have no problem sensing that as a 'full' turn, most drivers will want as free a steering wheel as possible.

Racing wheel suggestions

Thrustmaster T300RS

RRP: £310.00
Though it is designed for consoles, the T300RS is compatible with PCs and remains one of the best, sturdiest racing wheels you can buy. It offers a full 1,080-degree rotation angle, three pedals (most usually come with just two) and an adjustable pedal panel. This is for devoted racing enthusiasts only.

Logitech G29

RRP: £209.99
Replacing the incredibly popular G27 model that came before it, the G29 is an enhancement of what many consider to be one of the best racing wheels on the market. Sadly the gearstick is separate, but combine it with its LED readout to signify when a gear needs changing and the extra buttons for traction control and brake balancing and you'll have the ultimate racing setup.

Thrustmaster T-GT

RRP: £549.99
Again, this wheel is designed for the PlayStation (*Gran Turismo* will have that effect) but is compatible with PCs all the same. Only two pedals here but still a fairly robust and complete package all the same. A 1,080-degree rotation angle still offers a great amount of 'give' in the corners, but it's the force feedback that really impresses here with its subtle rumble.

Hori Apex

RRP: £89.99
Hori is a familiar name to fighting game fans, who swear by the company's arcade sticks. And in that sense, its cheaper racing wheel isn't going to be an option if you want a serious, enthusiast racing game experience. With its limited 270-degree turning angle, this is a controller that is better suited to arcade racers rather than the likes of *Forza*.

PART 5 Joysticks

There's been a resurgence of sorts in flight sims of late, with the likes of *Elite: Dangerous* and *Star Citizen* – among other non-spacefaring equivalents – really ramping up the need for a joystick. Of all the accessories and peripherals available, the joystick is perhaps the most antiquated, and as a result the most superfluous. But much like the effect racing wheels have on driving simulations, a good joystick can have a similar effect on flight simulations. It's certainly a purchase worth considering if you want to get truly suckered into *Elite: Dangerous* et al.

What to look for

Throttle control – This is a distinguishing feature between a good joystick and a bad one, giving you more incremental – and, importantly, tactile – control over your speed, and in the far reaches of space that counts for a lot in dogfights. You're going to want to favour a separate throttle control over something incorporated into the stick itself, but if you're after a budget option you likely won't get that.

Z-axis control – All joysticks will feature X- and Y-axis navigation, meaning left and right, forward and back. For the most part that will be enough, but if you want full control then you'll want to look for Z-axis control that allows you to twist the joystick clockwise or anti-clockwise to alter your craft's yaw, minimising the number of extra turns you'll need to make to face the right direction.

HOTAS – This stands for 'hands-on throttle and stick', and essentially means that the product you're buying comes with a dual-stick set-up – one for the throttle and one for navigational controls. You'll obviously need to pay more for the extra, but for a more realistic simulation experience having this as a feature will be extremely important.

Number of buttons – With the range of joysticks available on the market, it's easy to go too extreme in this regard. Either you'll have an excessive number of buttons – leading to over-complication and awkward use – or you'll have too few, leaving you reliant on having your keyboard by your side. Think about the game(s) you'd like to play with your joystick, and how many additional buttons you might need.

Joystick suggestions

Saitek X56 HOTAS

RRP: £219.99
The X56 has a build quality well worth its admittedly high price, plus twin throttles for control of dual-engine crafts and the addition of the all-important Z-axis control. You can even adjust the springs controlling the tension of the stick itself, so you can get a pressure that suits your taste.

Thrustmaster HOTAS Warthog

RRP: £349.99
This is perhaps excessively priced and since the set-up doesn't feature Z-axis control it feels like a bit of an unnecessary expense. But it is modelled on the real-world A-10C Thunderbolt II bomber, cased in metallic parts for a robust and realistic feel and features twin throttles and tons of extra buttons (that can be remapped to throttle control).

Thrustmaster T-Flight HOTAS X

RRP: £49.99
As an alternative to the Warthog, Thrustmaster has a great affordable option in the T-Flight HOTAS X set-up. It doesn't feature quite as many bells and whistles as the expensive equivalents, but it does have Z-axis control, which, as we keep saying, is an important feature to include, especially at such a low price.

Logitech Extreme 3D Pro

RRP: £44.99
The Extreme 3D Pro tends to sell for a lot less than its recommended price, making it one of the cheapest joysticks out there. It's also, for the money, one of the better low-end sticks, and though it does have a cheap feel to the buttons it is hard to knock what is an otherwise solid, budget-priced joystick. Perfect for smaller hands, too.

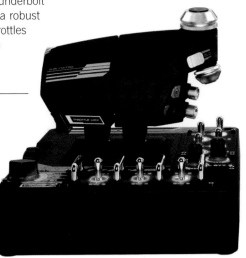

PART ⑤ Webcams

If you buy a laptop, you're almost guaranteed a webcam these days. It's something that most of us don't even think about. But on PC, the ability to share a video of yourself online to others whether for something as simple as a Skype call or something more technical like sharing footage of yourself gaming is actually something you'll need to put effort into thinking about. The webcam you choose comes down to the purpose you'll have for it, because there's certainly a wide variety to the extra features that can be bundled into these devices. Will you want a basic camera for conference calls, or do you want the best quality to appease your soon-to-be army of followers? Or do you even need one at all?

What to look for

Resolution and camera quality – Rule number one when buying a webcam is the resolution that it offers. These days clarity is everything, and that begins first and foremost with the quality of your camera's resolution. It's not the only thing to consider, of course, but so long as you're getting something with 1,080p or more then you'll have a device with high enough quality that the viewer won't have to strain to watch your video stream. In terms of quality of the camera itself, you'll need to check out reviews – perhaps even YouTube examples – of how well the lens can capture the realistic colours and white/black balancing of your room.

Field-of-view – The FOV of a camera changes from device to device, and some even have customisable ranges. This is important since this essentially dictates how much of you and

your background can be seen, so a wider FOV means that groups can be seen in the same shot. That might not be a necessity for you, but remember that you can always artificially crop the unwanted bits out of a video stream, you can't crop bits in. In that sense, an FOV of 60–75 is decent, but 90 is the one you want if you're after something wider.

Microphone – We've already mentioned in this section that a standalone microphone is necessary if you want to take gameplay streaming seriously, and in truth you're not likely to get a webcam with the microphone quality to compete with a dedicated peripheral just for that function. However, if you're starting out as a streamer or YouTuber and don't want to wear a headset while gaming, then a decent webcam with great quality audio capture will be ideal for you. Dual-microphone options or anything with high fidelity will always be advertised, so it shouldn't be hard to find.

Extra features – This is one of those things that is quite impossible to be specific about, because the list of bonus features in webcams is as long as the number of products. Some might have auto-focusing, low-light functionality, HDR or colour correction. Others might be wireless or allow for video capture of 60FPS. There may also be technical features like facial tracking or background removal – specifically for streaming, pretty much – while on-board processing reduces the additional load that video capture puts on your PC. In each case you don't only need to question how useful you'll find these features (to

help you overcome the jargon overload), but also find out how successful these extras are in doing what they set out to achieve.

Webcam suggestions

Logitech C920

RRP: £89.99
You'll actually get this webcam much cheaper than its retail price, which is an added bonus on top of an already pretty convincing package. The C920 is a great all-round camera and will be suitable for most any need thanks to its 1,080p resolution and 90-degree FOV. It offers great picture quality and low-light performance, and will work alongside Logitech's ChromaCam app that can be used to remove (or replace) the background automatically.

Razer Kiyo

RRP: £99.99
The Kiyo is no slouch in the video capture department thanks to its 1,080p resolution, 90-degree FOV, quick autofocusing and a very good level of image clarity. However, its unique selling point is also its most visible detail: the bright ring light that surrounds the camera lens to make for an unusual-looking device. It's great for increasing the saturation on your face – and as any model will tell you, that'll just make you look nicer – but it also means it'll work well in low-light situations.

Logitech BRIO

RRP: £199.99
This is about as high-end as a webcam can get, and its price alone might be enough to put anyone off. However, it's the only camera

capable of 4K resolution at the moment, which might be enough to sway your purchasing decision. With features like HDR support, digital zoom and a 90-degree FOV, it sort of earns back its value, though issues with autofocus can be a pain.

Microsoft LifeCam HD-3000

RRP: £23.99
For the budget option, the LifeCam HD-3000 is easily the choice to go for. It's the one that most businesses will pick because of its decent 720p resolution that is paired with great image quality, sharpness and colour reproduction. It's by no means the best in its class and you will easily find cameras that'll do better, but for the price there is nothing that can match this quality.

Virtual reality

One of the hot topics for gaming over the last few years has been that of virtual reality. Ever since Facebook bought out the leading VR developer, Oculus Rift, there's been an insurgence not only in competing products, but also interest from gamers and game developers alike. Though there have been a handful of attempts to make virtual reality mainstream since as early as the 80s, the tech is only now managing to reach a point where there are fewer technical restrictions on the hardware. This means that with the current suite of headsets you'll manage to achieve a believable VR experience to make your gaming more immersive and captivating than ever. But, what exactly is virtual reality?

The Oculus Rift and its spin-offs are the headsets that kick-started the surge in VR popularity, and since they have backing from Facebook they are likely to be the ones on top for a while.

While it's not exclusive to PC gaming, because of the high-end nature of the hardware it is something that is better suited to computers than the consoles, though Sony does have its own PlayStation-compatible headset. The current setup for VR (and this isn't likely to change any time soon), is a base computing platform that syncs up with a separate headset that you strap over your eyes. These bulky devices can look a little awkward to wear, but they're not so bad; they are essential to the experience, however, since they are built with motion detecting sensors that will track your head movements. These are then replicated in game, so if you look left for real then the character you're controlling will also look left.

This is typically combined with stereoscopic 3D, which means that the objects in the digital world will actually appear closer to you.

That's the basic idea. On top of this there are a handful of other things that complete the current state of the VR industry. Primary among these is the addition of controllers that track the movement of your hands, and typically this is considered to be almost mandatory for the true VR experience, although you could argue that a flight stick is going to be a better investment for something like *Elite: Dangerous*. With these motion-detecting controllers, however, you can feel yourself tactilely grab at objects or hold weapons, and since you're physically moving to interact with the world, you'll feel even more

immersed into the game. Other inputs include controller-free haptic controls – which work by detecting your movement in a given space – while there's even work being developed on smell-producing devices, too, to add an extra sense to the sensory gaming. And remember, VR isn't exclusive to gaming: given time (and Facebook's interest), virtual reality could function as social spaces, live sports shows, education or even art and design.

What games are available?

As you might expect for an experience about involving you directly into the game, virtual reality games are – for the largest part – first-person. Now there is a broad variety here since first-person viewpoints can fit into a number of genres, from shooters, racing games, platformers, puzzle games and even rhythm action games where you hit notes to the beat of the music. That last one, for example, includes a game called *Beat Saber*, which is essentially a game about swinging lightsabers to a funky beat; as you might expect, it's pretty fun. Alternatively, there are shooters like *Hover Junker* or the truly inventive *Superhot VR*, which has the novel gameplay mechanic of time only moving when you do, making for some cool bullet-dodging moments.

Racing games like *Dirt Rally* and flight simulators like *Elite: Dangerous* are particularly popular with VR due to the fact that you're

consigned to a cockpit, giving you the sense of speed and forward motion without the clumsiness of movement that can sometimes come from 'living' inside a VR world. There are naturally experiences that can only work in VR, too, and while we still haven't seen the very best of what virtual reality is capable of, there are already some interesting concepts. *Keep Talking and Nobody Explodes*, for example, is a hilarious game that has the headset wearer trying to defuse a bomb that only they can see with instructions from onlookers outside the virtual world. *Job Simulator* is capable of endless laughs, too, set in the near-future where

It might not tax your hardware very much, but *Superhot* is a must-play FPS – VR or not.

Dirt Rally is already one of the best rally racing games available, so the fact that there's a VR mode for cockpit view should really help to bring you into the tense races.

00:53.41

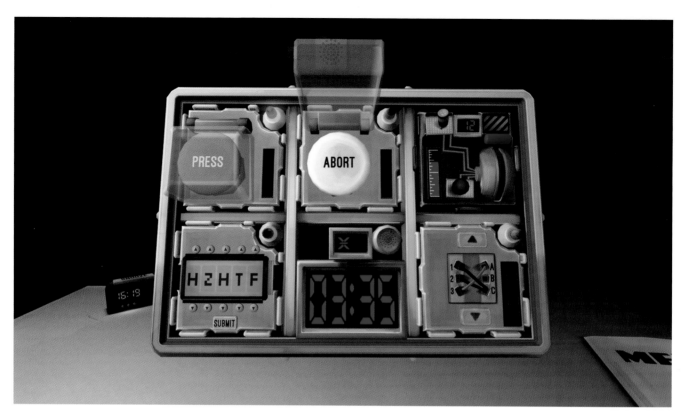

There are some really great uses of VR, such as this co-operative bomb defusal game where only the one wearing the headset can see the device.

It seems like such a simple use of VR, but digital recreations of board games means it's possible to play with friends even when everyone can't make it.

robots have replaced the workforce; here you play as a human – or at least their disembodied hands – as you try to relearn what it was like to have a job.

Then there's more experiential games, too, that aren't so much about the traditional 'gameplay' but rather about utilising the VR tech in immersive ways, whether that's the likes of roller coaster simulator *No Limits 2* or a digital recreation of the board game *Catan* with a 3D environment to sit around with friends as you play the resource trading game. Even Google Earth has a VR experience to make use of.

Being VR ready

Being immersed in virtual reality doesn't only happen with high-end, realistic graphics, but it can certainly help players feel more immersed in the worlds that are being rendered before their eyes. However, even outside of the hardware needed to render some of the visuals of these games, you're also having to compute the motion detection of the headsets as well as the stereoscopic 3D. They're not intensive additions, but you need to make sure you're prepared – and that means ensuring you have the hardware inside your machine to cope.

But the problem is that there's no real consistency to what is recommended. Oculus – the developer of the big name in the VR industry, the Oculus Rift – has its own minimum recommendations, but there are games whose own requirements surpass these. Numerous manufacturers and PC retailers also recommend different specs, so who's right? Well, the first thing to do is to follow the advice in our section about researching your build: if VR is important to you, then find out which games look interesting and build a system that will at least comfortably play those. However, there are still some expectations if you hope to play virtual reality games, including a certain number of ports that allow for all the cables. Luckily many GPUs – which are the powerhouses that will allow VR to work – will

advertise themselves as 'VR ready' these days, or at least have models devoted to that, so finding hardware you need without a guide is largely foolproof. Here's an example build that will see you able to play VR for a good few years:

Though these HaptX gloves aren't ready yet and do admittedly look a little monstrous, haptic glove technology could be used in conjunction with VR for a fully immersive experience.

Minimum specs	Recommended specs
• GPU with 4GB memory • i3 CPU with 3.6GHz speed • 8GB RAM • 1x USB 3.0 port, 2x USB 2.0 ports • 64-bit operating system (Windows 10) • HDMI 1.3 video output	• GPU with 6GB (NVIDIA) or 8GB (AMD) memory • i7 CPU with 3.7GHz speed • 16GB RAM • 3x USB 3.0 ports, 1x USB 2.0 • 64-bit operating system (Windows 10) • HDMI 1.3 video output

HTC is the other big headset producer, and has made great strides in combating Oculus.

PART

Overclocking your gaming PC

Overclocking is a bit of a scary-sounding phrase. To those who don't know the rules of engagement it just sounds dangerous. Those who do know of overclocking, but have never done it, are likely put off by the stories and they've heard the seriousness with which the phrase is often used. Overclocking is seen as the reserve of elite PC enthusiasts, but in truth it's not too difficult to do – and when done properly it's not nearly as risky as you might imagine.

Overclocking lets you access more power from your processor, graphics card and even memory by overriding their factory settings and tinkering with them to best optimise them for your own PC hardware and set-up. It can mean squeezing the very best performance out of your system, or enhancing older parts so that they last a little bit longer. Understanding overclocking means you can make the most out of your gaming PC, and it's a helpful way of saving on upgrades or the initial budget.

Since overclocking does mean you're tampering with the base optimal settings, it will mean those parts will run hotter, and higher temperatures can lead to failing hardware – and not only the parts that you've overclocked. Yet remember that these factory settings are often set quite a bit lower than they need to be, making the out-of-the-box hardware you buy for your PC more likely to be compatible with a wide range of PCs and suffer fewer faults as a result. In the eyes of the manufacturer it's better to be safe than sorry, so don't let the potential issues put you off. That's not to say you shouldn't be careful, of course: it's a gradual

process of incremental upgrades, and if you are interested in attempting to supercharge your PC then you need to do so in small stages with regular tests. In that sense it can be a bit of a laborious task, but much like the thrill of putting together your first gaming PC the sensation of reaching new and better benchmarking tests can be enough of a thrill to get enthusiasts interested.

To help you get your head around overclocking your hardware we've detailed everything you need to know to assist in your own overclocking adventures. Since every piece of hardware is different, there's no sure-fire, step-by-step method to unlocking your PC's full potential, but as long as you have the knowledge to follow the process without any concern then you'll soon find it's not nearly as scary as it first sounds. We'll also document some of the best, most useful pieces of software you'll need for benchmarking – the process of stress-testing your PC to ensure your changes are safe – and some of the most popular games and applications overclockers like to use to show off just how powerful their PCs really are.

Every BIOS will look different, from older blue screen styles like this to more modern, higher resolution options – often with black screens.

```
 CMOS Setup Utility - Copyright (C) 1984-2011 Award Software

  ▶ MB Intelligent Tweaker(M.I.T.)      Load Fail-Safe Defaults

  ▶ Standard CMOS Features               Load Optimized Defaults

  ▶ Advanced BIOS Features               Set Supervisor Password

  ▶ Integrated Peripherals               Set User Password

  ▶ Power Management Setup               Save & Exit Setup

  ▶ PC Health Status                     Exit Without Saving


  Esc : Quit                  ↑↓→←: Select Item     F11 : Save CMOS to BIOS
  F8  : Q-Flash               F10 : Save & Exit Setup  F12 : Load CMOS from BIOS

                    Change CPU's Clock & Voltage
```

PART  Understanding overclocking

Before you actually jump into the overclocking itself, it is important that you first understand the technical side of what it is you're trying to achieve. Every piece of hardware is different; one part could be minutely different to another of the exact same make and model due to the manufacturing process, so it's important to know what you're changing and what effect that change has. To help we're going to explain some of the terms you'll need to understand when overclocking – that way you won't have any problems when overclocking your own system. And since you can enhance the performance of parts such as your graphics card, processor and memory, we'll try to keep this section as general as possible across all forms of overclocking.

Key terms to learn

Overclocking – Let's start with the phrase itself, which is fairly self-explanatory. Overclocking is the process of increasing the clock speed of a particular piece of PC hardware to run faster than its initial factory settings, unlocking performance gains. Additionally this can mean increasing the voltage that piece of hardware accepts to help it attain higher speeds.

BIOS – This is the set-up screen where you'll do your adjustments to the hardware – the actual process of overclocking itself. This is essentially the software hardwired into your motherboard, and lets you control the system's hardware and how it performs. You may have seen the BIOS before or you may not have needed to, but either way it is always accessed immediately after starting the system up.

Clock – With all this mention of 'clocks' you're probably asking 'What is a clock?' Well, this is the microchip inside your computer that regulates timing, that vibrates when electricity is applied. It is measured in hertz, with a 2.0GHz processor capable of two billion cycles – or vibrations – a second. It is often represented in your BIOS as 'BCLK'. This is your base clock speed, and is used to calculate your CPU's overall speed: so if your system has a base clock of 100MHz (perhaps shown as slightly under that) with a CPU multiplier or ratio of 30 then your CPU will have a total speed of

3,000MHz, or 3.0GHz. Increasing the multiplier to 33 will make your CPU a 3.3GHz processor.

Data buses – There are multiple buses inside your computer, but the most important is the main one connecting your CPU to the rest of the system. It is the communication interface that transfers data from your processor to the rest of your PC's hardware, so essentially its speed affects how fast the other parts of your computer can be given commands from the CPU. These can come in various forms, but the function is always the same. Older processors call this the frontside bus (or FSB), while more recent terms include AMD's EV6 or Intel's QuickPath Interconnect. Though these don't all work in exactly the same way, they do control the processing of information and so are pivotal to understand when overclocking.

Clock multiplier/ratio – Otherwise known as CPU multiplier, bus/core ratio or internal multiplayer, this is the number of times the processor's own internal clock completes a cycle within every external clock count. This is used to calculate the total speed of your processor by multiplying the clock multiplier with the external clock's speed. It is one of the first numbers you'll want to try and adjust in the overclocking process.

Voltage – This is an extra side to overclocking that is important to understand. While increasing the voltage supply to a particular piece of

If you want to achieve the very best graphics from your games, overclocking can be a good option for achieving that with cheaper or mid-range parts.

hardware won't actually increase its performance – much like putting extra fuel into a car – it is often a necessity as you increase the speed of that component. The faster an overclocked part runs the more power it's going to need to function at its best. As with the overclocking process, this should be done slowly and incrementally, to ensure the right voltage is set.

Benchmarking – This is a process whereby you will monitor your PC – often under stress-test situations – to ensure that the upgrade you have made to a piece of hardware has both been successful and isn't likely to cause any damage to your hardware. Even outside of overclocking, benchmarking is a useful way of discovering just how powerful your PC is. Since there is a risk of permanent damage to your components by overclocking, it's imperative that you use benchmarking to ensure you haven't exceeded any boundaries. We'll talk in more depth about benchmarking and the software you can use later in this chapter.

DirectX – When it comes to graphics cards, you'll often see the term DirectX pop up –

often seen as DX9 or DX11. This is an API that a lot of modern games rely on to function, and though it's not a prerequisite for PC gaming a large portion of games do need a compatible graphics card to function well. Thankfully your only concern is whether or not you're running a DX9 or a DX11 card. DX11 is a more recent, up-to-date and powerful version of DirectX, and enables a lot of fancy extras within games, and most recent GPUs are powerful enough to handle DX11. Make sure you know which yours is, however, before going about overclocking, as it'll help you understand which games you're best testing it with.

Preparation

Before you actually start overclocking there are a few things you'll want to consider first. This will mean downloading and installing some software to help monitor your changes – and stress-test those that you have made – as well as consider some of the hardware requirements for overclocking. This latter part might not be relevant to you, but it's worth knowing about if it is something you want to do in the future.

CPU-Z/GPU-Z – This is a very handy piece of software that details your system's various values, such as clock speed, voltage and so on. It's good to run prior to any changes you make and then again after to first ensure that the changes have been maintained properly but also to check that the settings you've altered are working correctly. The equivalent software for when you come to overclock your graphics card is called GPU-Z.

Stress-test software – There's a wide variety of stress-test software available, and it differs with the type of hardware you're overclocking. We'll talk about them in closer detail in each specific section, but for CPU stress-testing you're looking for the likes of Prime95, BurnInTest, FurMark or AIDA64. There are plenty more you can use, but if you're concerned then by all means use a combination of different stress-test software – we can't emphasise enough the importance of making sure your changes won't damage your hardware. For GPU overclocking it's a little simpler, but the easiest to recommend is FutureMark's 3DMark.

Real Temp – Since there's a point to all this stress-testing, you're going to need software to run alongside it. Real Temp will let you monitor the true temperature of all your hardware components to ensure that they aren't overheating during the stress test.

Cooling – If all you're doing is making small upgrades through overclocking then you might not need to worry too much about cooling. As long as your system has enough ventilation and a cooling system suitable for the hardware you have, then smaller changes to the hardware will likely pass without having to change your cooling. In fact, the stock CPU fan should be enough to slightly bump up your processor's power. That's not to say you shouldn't keep an eye on the heat of your system, because that's the biggest threat when overclocking. If you want to make bigger changes then you'll definitely need to make sure that the higher temperature of your computer and its parts are being rectified.

Power supply – It's highly unlikely that you'll need to upgrade your power supply, but since you will be increasing the voltage your parts

are using during the overclocking process then the overall power your machine will need will increase too. Chances are you'll have a PSU installed that more than adequately supplies your machine, but if you've got a lower supply of power and find your machine isn't running sufficiently after the overclocking process, it could be that you'll need to upgrade the PSU.

Overclocking compatibility – Not all motherboards, or indeed processors and graphics cards, are suitable for overclocking. Some manufacturers prefer to keep things locked down, while others unlock the potential of their hardware for enthusiasts by default. Thankfully, most high-end PC gaming components are built with overclocking in mind, though you do tend to pay a premium for them.

CPU-Z and GPU-Z help you to monitor your system's processor and graphics card respectively to ensure that your overclocking changes are functioning.

PART

Overclocking your CPU

CPU overclocking is the most common form of enhancement, but when it comes to gaming you might actually want to overclock your graphics card instead since it handles a large portion of how the game actually looks. The CPU handles computational commands, however, so if you want to improve the speed with which processing is handled then it's the CPU you want to upgrade. It's worth remembering that not all hardware is the same, and that even the exact same components could differ in terms of theoretical maximum – even experienced overclockers need to follow the incremental process. Certain makes and models of hardware are better suited towards overclocking, too, though these days modern parts are a little more open in that regard. With so many variants in hardware, it's impossible to give a definitive step-by-step process when it comes to overclocking. However, the changes you make are generally the same; just remember to be careful, methodical and incremental about the changes you do make. And always stress-test each subtle change.

When overclocking your processor you're going to be spending a large portion of time in your BIOS. It looks intimidating, so have a poke around – you can always exit without making changes.

1. Test the machine

First things first: you're going to want to know what your machine is capable of unchanged. This will give you a solid base for knowing how your machine should be running once you've changed the settings. Using the software suggested previously, such as Prime95 alongside CPU-Z and Real Temp, stress-test the machine. Make a note of the figures you're reaching, both unstressed and stressed. It might seem unimportant, but this will help you to know whether an overclocked part is functioning well.

2. Access the BIOS

After you've got the details for the machine in its default state, you'll want to start the process of overclocking. Reboot your system and, as it starts up, press the correct key to initiate the BIOS screen. This differs between motherboards, often requiring you to press the 'delete' key when prompted or one of the 12 function keys at the top of the keyboard. A screen with the motherboard's manufacturer's name will appear, and it is often here that you'll be told which button to press to load the BIOS system set-up screen. Failing that, take a look inside your motherboard's manual – it'll tell you in there.

3. Find the CPU frequency settings

What you're looking for is the list of settings that control how the CPU functions. Again this differs between processors and motherboards,

so you'll need to search around the BIOS for these settings. Look for CPU frequencies, BCLK or base clock speeds, multipliers and ratios or some of the other terms detailed in the 'Key terms to learn' section. You can also refer to your motherboard manual to find the section you need when overclocking. At this point don't change anything, just take note of some of the default settings and confirm you're looking at the right screen.

4. Adjust the CPU settings

Once you're feeling confident, you can begin by adjusting the settings of the CPU. This should be a very incremental process. While it's good to search online for some example settings other users have achieved through overclocking – and in this regard you should always take an average, rather than a maximum – to give you a good idea of what you might be able to reach, remember that all parts are different. Even if you're certain of the numbers you'll be able to reach, you should still go through the process gradually to ensure that your hardware is overclocked safely.

5. Increase the multiplier

You should start by changing your CPU's multiplier – though this might actually be termed clock ratio in your BIOS. This base setting could be anywhere between 15 and 35, depending on the base clock speed (BCLK) of your system. By increasing the multiplier/ratio, you're effectively increasing the number of cycles the processor

Where your particular motherboard stores the CPU frequency settings differs from board to board. Some will bundle it all in one screen, others within separate menus.

When it comes to multi-core processors, you may be able to unlock the ability to customise the frequency of your CPU depending on how many of the cores are active.

completes each second. It might be tempting to simply select the highest number, but don't – this would likely be disastrous for your CPU. Instead increase the number by only one or two points. As we've said, it is safer to make these changes slowly, testing all the while. Additionally it's worth noting that some set-ups will allow you to specify individual multipliers depending on how many CPU cores are in use – Intel calls this Turbo Boost mode. If you prefer to tailor your system that way, you'll need to enable the mode and specify individual multipliers for when one, two, three and four of the CPU's cores are active, scaling downwards to allow for optimum use. After the changes save the settings and restart the system, booting into Windows. If your system is locked and not well suited to overclocking then you may not be able to adjust the multiplier, and in that case you'll need to adjust the base clock speed instead, but we'll talk about that soon. It's much better to change a single setting each time rather than make multiple BIOS changes at once – this will help you diagnose a problem if your system throws faults after the changes. It's handy to write down the different changes you make, allowing you to better keep track of the numbers and readjust to a previous functioning setting in case of faults.

6. Stress test
After making a change in the BIOS and rebooting you then need to ensure the settings have stuck and that they are safe for your system. To begin with keep an eye on the system start-up for anything unusual: any errors will give you a sure sign the change caused a problem, as will forced reboots, but is the

system taking especially long to start up? It shouldn't and this might be a sign that there is a problem. Once at the Windows screen, boot up CPU-Z to ensure that the changed settings have been made, then start up your choice of stress-test software. Remember that gaming is one of the most taxing functions a PC can do – at least 3D games – so it might in fact be better to run a combination of stress-test software to make sure your system is safe at full load. Pairing up the likes of BurnInTest and FurMark is a good, and fairly quick, way of ensuring your CPU and GPU can handle the increase in power. Remember to run Real Temp too to ensure that your system isn't reaching dangerous temperatures. Even with this stress-test software, you might want to consider running a high-end, graphically intensive game (we have some examples later in the chapter) to ensure that the upgrade is safe. If the game locks up, freezes, stutters, crashes or you find your system getting far too hot then you'll know something needs to be done.

7. In case of faults
If there is any kind of fault during this process then before repeating the stage again you'll need to find the reason for this fault and rectify it. The faults you come across could include forced restarts or shutdowns, failed stress-tests, unexpected error messages during start-up or failing or erratic running of games. This is likely caused by one of two things: either your increased strain is causing the processor to overheat, thus forcing your PC to shut down as a failsafe measure or it could be that the processor is not getting enough power to run the adjustment. It's likely that early on in the overclocking process the lack of power will be the problem, in which case you'll need to adjust the voltage going to your processor (next step). It could make sense to readjust the change you made to its previous figure to make sure that the fault was caused by this change; if it still occurs at this point, there may be a bigger problem with your PC or individual components.

8. Increase the voltage
With a small change it's unlikely that you'll need to increase the voltage supply, but if your stress-testing does raise problems then it's likely that the upgraded CPU isn't getting enough power to let the improvement function. To do this you'll need to once again head into your BIOS and look for the voltage settings, often referred to as 'Vcore' and usually in a different menu. As with before it will differ depending on your motherboard, but there will be a setting for CPU/Core voltage somewhere in there. You

don't need to adjust the voltage settings by much at a time, and again it should always be a gradual upgrade – more voltage going into the component will increase its running temperature so you want to be very conservative with your changes. A voltage increase of 0.0500 at a time is often enough, but remember to keep an eye on the CPU temperature after each tweak you make. As before, save the voltage change and stress-test the machine again.

9. Repeat the process

This is the easiest way of overclocking your CPU, and providing your parts are open to overclocking you should have no problems following it from here. Repeat the process of slowly increasing the multiplier/clock ratio and the core voltage, stress-testing as you go until you have a setting you're happy with. As you increase the voltage remember to keep an eye on the running temperature of your CPU. A maximum of 85°C is generally considered safe, but always search online for the right temperature for your processor. And remember that the higher the temperature and the harder you run your components the more likely you are to decrease their lifespan – like anything that gets excessive use, really. It's not always better to overclock your machine until it is needed for this reason.

10. Increasing the clock speed

If you've got locked components then you won't be able to adjust the multiplier/clock ratio through the BIOS, but that doesn't mean you can't still overclock. You may still be able to subtly increase the base clock to maximise your potential gains. This can cause a greater strain on your system as a whole, especially as adjusting the base clock can also have

a knock-on effect with other components – such as the various data buses transferring information between each part – and these may not work well with increased speeds, so exercise a lot of caution when making these changes. To adjust the clock speed you need to once again enter the BIOS and look for the CPU frequencies menu – most likely in the same menu or submenu where you found the multiplier/clock ratio options. Look for the reference to your base clock speed: in Intel chips you're probably looking for 'BCLK', but in AMD chips you may be adjusting the data bus instead, so look for 'FSB' or something similar. Your motherboard manual will have all the details you need. As with the multiplier you want to slowly increase the speed at which the base clock speed performs (measured in MHz), save the settings and then reboot the system into Windows to stress-test. The increments by which it can be increased won't be too vast, and that's for the best – as always, slow and steady is preferred here.

11. Move on to GPU or RAM

Once you've settled on a speed and running standard for your CPU, you may be hungry to adjust even more of your PC. Remember that you can always enable multi-core overclocking on some quad-core chips, and that will give you even greater control – especially when it comes to games, since rarely are all four cores of a chip used in computation for games. After that you'll likely want to overclock your graphics card, which will, in most cases, be bearing the brunt of your PC's computation when it comes to games. Even your RAM can be overclocked, enabling it to run at the speed it is intended to, since most memory is actually underclocked initially.

There's a wide range of stress-testing software available. Prime95 shown here is good for overall system tests, great for overclocking your CPU or RAM.

PART **6**

Overclocking your graphics card

While overclocking your processor is certain to help your PC handle more demanding tasks and is one of the first things you'll think of when overclocking your PC, the graphics card should perhaps be the first target of overclocking for PC gamers. These days the GPU is the piece of hardware that handles the bulk of processing when it comes to 3D gaming, so if you want to make your games look as good or play as smoothly as possible – especially if you've gone for a cheaper option to save overall costs on your build – then you'll want to follow these steps. Thankfully it's a little easier to do than with a CPU, though the elements you'll be changing are largely the same. It can be handled in Windows through dedicated GPU overclocking software, so it's much less arduous when changing different factors. As with CPU overclocking, however, every GPU is different, even between otherwise identical makes and models, so you should make small changes at a time, testing them with benchmarking software as you do.

1. Install the drivers

Most GPU software these days will prompt you when a new, non-beta, version of your graphics card's drivers are available, but even if they don't then it's often better to install the latest drivers before you start overclocking your GPU. You'll find these on either the manufacturer's website or the brand's website, allowing you to download and install the most recent software available. In some cases you may be able to download beta drivers as soon as they're available, which is something some gamers do to get the absolute most out of their GPUs – when it comes to overclocking, however, avoid doing this since these beta drivers can sometimes be unstable. Having the most recent, non-beta drivers will give your GPU the absolute best compatibility with your own system and the games you will play.

2. Benchmark your GPU

As with CPU overclocking, you want to start by finding out what your graphics card is capable of. There is a lot of potential benchmarking software to use so we've dedicated a section to it; if you don't know which software to use, take a look at that to get a better idea of what you might want to download. As with stress-

testing, this will push your graphics card to the maximum, testing its ability to render models, calculate lighting and even its control of physics. Different benchmarking software works in different ways, but the result is the same – to find out how well your GPU performs. Run the benchmarking software and take a note of your GPU's default performance.

3. Run MSI Afterburner

Since GPU overclocking can be done with Windows software there are, as you might expect, a large number of options open to you. For the sake of ease, however, we're going to suggest using MSI Afterburner, which is easy to use and provides a uniform experience for most graphics cards. You're welcome to find and download your own preferred option, but this is the most robust and most widely used option available. AMD cards come with Catalyst Control Center, which enables a similar set of functions if you prefer a safer option, however MSI Afterburner also allows control over the voltage of your card for maximum overclocking potential.

4. Adjust the clock speed

Look for the clock speed setting in MSI Afterburner. It'll be a slider bar with 'min' on

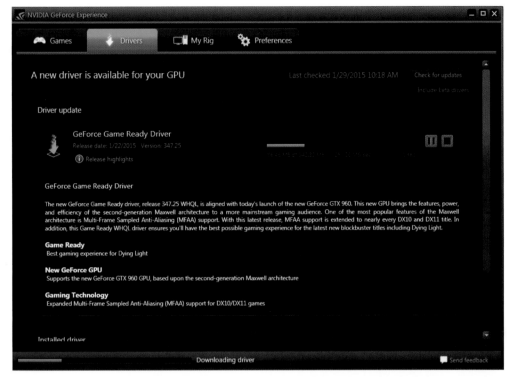

It's always good to keep your drivers up to date, especially if you want to get the most from recent games. It's imperative you do it before overclocking, however.

one end and 'max' on the other. As ever you want to avoid sliding it up to the maximum, since that could just overload your card and potentially cause damage. Firstly, if there is also a Shader Clock speed then you want to link this to the Core Clock speed too, which is done with the button on the right-hand side in MSI Afterburner. You'll want to adjust the two simultaneously for the best results. Just increase the clock speed by a small amount – 10MHz at a time is enough – then apply the changed setting ahead of benchmarking. If you're using MSI Afterburner you'll want to save these settings to one of the software's profiles, a function that lets you toggle between overclocked changes – a great option if you want to protect your GPU's lifespan.

5. Benchmark the changes

Now you'll want to test the changes you've made, but first boot up GPU-Z to ensure that the changes to the settings have successfully been applied. Once you've confirmed the changes, run your benchmark software of choice to find out how it compares with your previous test, all the while keeping an eye on the temperature of your graphics card. If you have a high-end GPU then you shouldn't encounter many problems during the benchmark after your first overclocking change. If you have a medium- or low-end card then you may notice some frame-rate issues (most benchmarking software ramps up the demand later on in the test), but so long as the test completes successfully, doesn't get too hot and provides you with a clear improvement then you can consider the change a success.

6. Repeat the clock speed increase

If your benchmarking was a success then you can repeat the process of increasing your GPU's clock speed at 10MHz at a time. It's good to research your particular graphics card to find out what sort of figures most people have achieved to give you a good idea of what you can aim for, but don't let that tempt you into pushing up the numbers quickly; to reiterate, every card is different and yours might not achieve the same overclocking changes as another. Keep gradually increasing the clock speed until your benchmarking causes a problem: your graphics card driver might crash, the screen might go black or graphical artefacts might appear during the benchmarking. Additionally your card may be reaching intolerable temperatures, which will cause permanent damage if left in that

131

state. At this point you've gone past the current maximum for your GPU and you should reduce it back down to the last successful clock speed.

7. Increase the voltage

If you're using MSI Afterburner or other software that allows the adjustment of voltage to your GPU then at this point you can try and further your graphics card's capabilities. Be aware that increasing the voltage to your GPU will increase the temperature it runs at, as well as put the card under greater duress – meaning its lifespan could be decreased. Though it will allow you to reach greater clock speeds, if you're not willing to risk your graphics card in this way, you can skip this step. To adjust the voltage of your GPU you'll first need to unlock the feature. In MSI Afterburner that means going into the settings and looking for the 'Unlock Voltage Control' option. Once done you can then adjust the

voltage as you did with the core clock; each card controls voltage at its own increments, so type in an increase of 10mV and the software will automatically scale it to the right amount. With this extra power you can now try and readjust the clock speed as you did in step six, gradually increasing it by 10MHz each time and running your benchmark software to ensure the change has been safe. Once you begin to see problems in the benchmarking process again, increase the voltage by another 10mV and repeat the process. When increasing your voltage make sure you know what the safe maximum voltage of your graphics card is, as you absolutely do not want to exceed that. Additionally you need to pay extra attention to the temperature increasing – 80°C is considered safe, while 90°C is generally considered excessive, but remember to search online for the safe maximum temperature for your card.

It's important to test each change you make to ensure it has both been a success and won't damage your graphics card in the process.

8. Increase the memory clock speed

Once you've found a safe overclock that you're happy with, you can then repeat the process for the GPU's memory clock speed. This is the exact same process as the GPU clock-speed increase, except you're altering the memory clock-speed slider instead. As before a process of gradual alterations, GPU-Z checks and benchmark tests will be important to find the perfect maximum. It's perhaps safer to take a note of your new GPU clock speed and voltage settings and reset them to the defaults before changing the GPU memory clock speed. Then, if all goes well, use the new settings for GPU clock speed, voltage and GPU memory clock speed to see how it all works together. As always only change one setting at a time so you can easily resolve a problem should you encounter one. You're not going to notice quite as many gains from increasing the memory clock speed, but it's still beneficial in order to get the most out of your GPU.

9. Test it out

Once you've found overclocked settings that you're happy with, and benchmarking tells you they are safe, the important thing to do is to test it all out. Boot up some graphically intensive games to ensure that your settings are safe in a 'real' situation. While benchmarking is great for finding the potential maximum, the added dynamism of gaming can often cause greater stress that the predictability of benchmarking software fails to replicate. If you ever get any issues with your graphics card while playing games – such as regular GPU drivers crashing or black screens – then you should readjust your overclocked settings a little, lowering them and retesting to ensure everything is safe for your GPU. And, as always, keep an eye on those temperatures.

You can use any other software that enables GPU overclocking functionality, but MSI Afterburner is particularly easy to use for practically any make and model of graphics card.

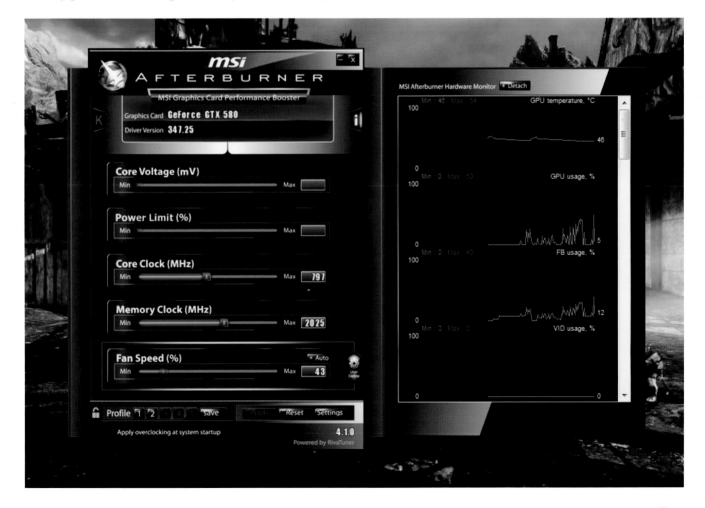

PART  # Overclocking your memory

With so many different types and grades of RAM, and even varying sizes and capabilities within each type, it can be something of a minefield trying to navigate the complications of overclocking your system's memory. Add in the fact that some parts are considerably better suited to overclocking than others and the fact that the performance gains are comparatively small, and it can seem a somewhat fruitless task. All the same, if you are looking to squeeze every last ounce out of your PC then you may feel you want to manually reconfigure your RAM settings to get your money's worth. But because of all these varying factors, it's not suitable for a step-by-step guide to overclocking your RAM; instead we'll presume you have at least tweaked your CPU settings (since you'll want to do that first anyway), so you've already experienced your system's BIOS. Here then we're going to detail some of the things you need to look out for when overclocking your memory, and explain how you can go about doing it.

Key things to know

Testing software – As with any form of overclocking, it's always good to test the changes you've made. When it comes to RAM it's a little trickier to test, of course, but there is software that can help. First you'll want to make use of CPU-Z, as you have with overclocking the processor, while Prime95 is a good overall system stress-tester. Specifically for RAM, though, you can download testing software such as MaxMem or SiSoftware's Sandra, which will check the memory for its new potential.

Frequency – Most commonly referred to as the DRAM frequency, this is the speed at which your RAM is capable of running. It'll say the speed your memory will be able to run at on the packaging, in the RAM's product description, or even printed on the label on the RAM itself. It is measured in MHz from very low-end at 333MHz to 2,400MHz and over. It's a large part of what affects how quickly your RAM can send and receive data. You'll find this option in your BIOS and it can be adjusted to better match what your RAM is expected to achieve, but remember all hardware is different – even if you have increased your RAM frequency to the number it says on the label, you may still

encounter problems and will have to lower it slightly. As ever, the faster it will run the more strain you'll be putting it under, so it's better to find your maximum RAM frequency and drop it down a single setting to maintain reliable regular use from your memory. Also remember that your memory will be limited by what your FSB is capable of – and as we discussed in the CPU section, that can often be changed manually. If you want to know more, read the next point.

FSB:DRAM – In CPU-Z you'll see this figure, which is the FSB to DRAM frequency ratio. Associated with the point on frequency above, it tells you how fast one part is running with regard to the other. Your RAM will always be limited by the speed of your FSB, so you want to try and have that ratio as close to 1:1 as possible – if the FSB is faster than your memory then you're going to get a bottleneck, and the speed of your RAM will limit the FSB. Alternatively it is not necessarily worse to have the RAM running faster than the FSB, because while the latter will bottleneck the former the way your memory accesses data (and its purpose in a

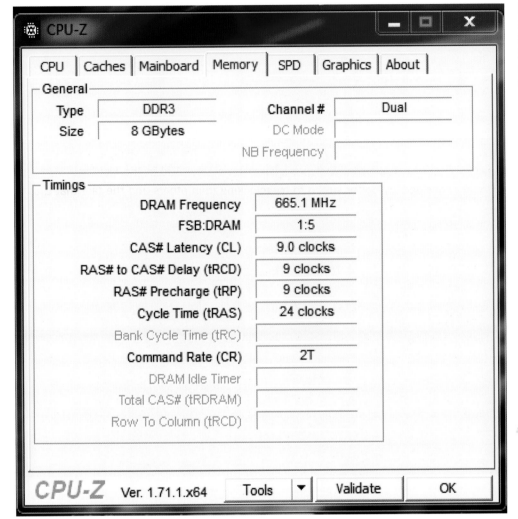

computer system anyway) will mean it being faster is not really a negative. Where possible try to make sure your FSB:DRAM ratio is either 1:1 or has the larger number on the right-hand side.

RAM timings – The second most important number for your memory is its set of timings, often advertised as 'CAS' (Column Address Strobe) or 'CAS Latency' even though the latter is technically inaccurate. There are a variety of different timings, but there are four key figures to look out for. These can be found on the label on the RAM itself, and are usually styled with four different digits separated by a dash, for example: 13-15-15-28. These timings represent the various delays that your RAM will be put under

when handling data, so the lower the number the better. While it might be advertised at these timings, it might be capable of much shorter delays. Using CPU-Z and the RAM timings given earlier as a guide, the four figures you're looking to change are:

CAS Latency (CL), in this case 13

RAS# to CAS# Delay (tRCD), in this case the first 15

RAS# Precharge (tRP), in this case the second 15

Cycle Time (tRAS), in this case 28

Lowering RAM timings – While we could explain what these timings do and what they affect, that in itself is not too important;

The four timing figures you need to change for overclocking your RAM are CAS Latency, tRCD, tRP and tRAS. That's the order they will appear in, too.

instead we'll explain how to proceed to lower the timings. In the BIOS you want to look for the DRAM timing configuration, looking for the four different timings referenced in the point above. As always this should be a staged process as you discover the lowest delay you can apply to these settings, changing one setting at a time, saving and then testing your change once back in Windows. You can use the base timings as a guide for what kind of ratio each timing can be lowered to – so in our example the CL of 13 would end up at a lower number than the tRCD and tRP. The Cycle Time (or tRAS) will always be higher than the rest. There's a lot more manipulation involved with memory overclocking than the likes of CPU or GPU overclocking, so be prepared for a lot of system restarts. If your PC fails to boot then the last setting you changed was too low.

Command Rate (CR) – You'll basically get two numbers for this, either 1T or 2T. 1T is always faster than 2T, but the increase in performance is marginal at best, so you may not feel the need to change it since running it at 2T is more stable. If you are looking to maximise every aspect of your PC, however, and providing your memory is capable of running 1T, then this can be a quick and easy change to make. You'll find the option in your BIOS with the rest of the memory options.

Voltage – As with all hardware, increasing the voltage will allow you to increase the frequency, or speed, at which it runs. And, as with all hardware, it's important to remember that increasing the voltage will also increase the risk of damage to the component. The risk is greater for RAM, however, since there is no innate fail-safe to protect the component from damage, such as forced shut-offs like with your CPU and GPU. This means you have to be especially careful if you want to increase the voltage of your RAM; find out what the 'right' setting for your memory is, as well as what its absolute maximum is. If you want to be careful then use very conservative voltage increases if at all.

SPD – Serial Presence Detect is a way for manufacturers to supply a set of viable changes to the memory. These are built into the RAM itself, and under software such as CPU-Z you can find out what settings your memory is capable of. It's a handy guide to understanding the best way to go about altering your timings in the BIOS since it will give you an idea of the range – lowest and highest – that the memory is capable of. Don't take it as fact, of course, since

you can still tweak it to how you like, but it's good to check before any changes are made.

XMP settings – This is related to the SPD settings. As an alternative to JEDEC standard settings that are supplied with most memory, you can also get XMP settings. These are prescribed profiles for the RAM itself, which can be enabled in the BIOS to automatically overclock your memory for you. It's a safer option for those inexperienced or wary of overclocking memory since it will give the safe timings and frequency settings as designed by the manufacturer. Once you're more comfortable with overclocking, however, you might want to forgo this option in favour of your own tweaking to find the very best setting for your system. You can find these XMP settings in the SPD tab of CPU-Z.

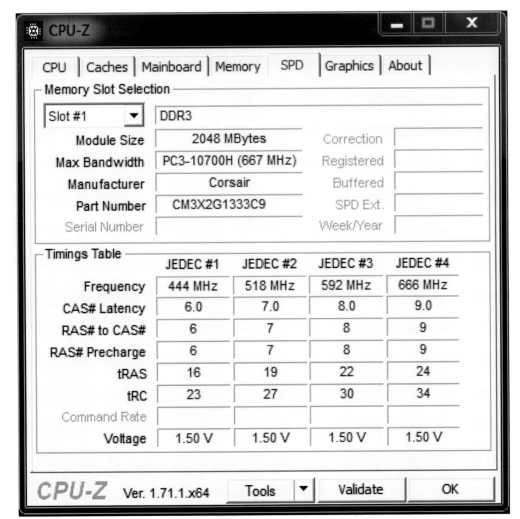

If you're not sure where to begin when it comes to RAM timing changes, you can check with the manufacturer's in-built SPD settings to see what kinds of ranges they suggest.

PART **6**

Benchmarking and testing

It's important to remember that overclocking is a very gradual process, and even the most experienced overclockers must go through a regime of tweaking and testing to find the setting that they're most comfortable with. While overclocking can initially be quite a daunting task, providing you're vigilant about regular stress-tests and benchmarking then you'll deal easily with problems as they arise, and know exactly what previous state to revert to in order to make it work again. When overclocking your GPU, however, you've a number of benchmarking options available, and we wanted to devote some space to talking about the different software and why you might favour one over another. You should also remember that while an overclock might be 'benchmark stable', it might not be suitable when it comes to gaming. This is especially the case with GPUs, where the extra variable from your own input can put more strain on its calculations and processing. We've included some good suggestions for you to test your overclocked GPU, should you need it.

Benchmarking software

Futuremark 3DMark

3DMark is perhaps the most professional of the variants of benchmarking software, and as such it has made something of a name for itself as the go-to tool to test your system. 3DMark is designed specifically for 3D gaming, however, and will test everything from your GPU's ability to render models to how well it computes physics, lighting, particle effects and even other modern gaming techniques like volumetric fog. It's about as comprehensive as you can get, though lower-end cards will begin to struggle with frame rate towards the end. It'll even give you a calculated 3DMark 'score' upon completion, showing where your current system ranks in the grand scheme of things.

Unigine Heaven

The second most common benchmarking software is Unigine's Heaven, and it perhaps loses out to 3DMark due to the fact that its free, basic version isn't quite as feature-packed as 3DMark. All the same, it's probably best to run each of these individually once you think you've

settled on an overclock you're comfortable with just to ensure that you're getting results you can be pleased with. Both test the same elements, so it's really down to personal preference which you use when it comes to regular tests in between overclocking changes.

FRAPS

There are two versions of FRAPS, free and paid-for. While the fairly cheap cost of the software brings with it some added benefits – especially if you hope to capture raw video footage – the free version is worth downloading for your own tests. It's worth noting that this isn't actually benchmarking software; instead it will display an up-to-date frame-rate counter over the games you play, making it imperative that you use this software while testing the capabilities of your GPU by playing the games themselves. Some players even get quite finicky about their frame rates and like to always keep it active while playing. It's a low demand on the system, so there's really no reason not to.

3DMark is the most popular benchmarking software, and rightly so. It stress-tests your GPU in every respect, from rendering to physics and lighting, as well as providing a 3DMark score for easy-to-understand ratings of where your GPU stands.

Unigine doesn't offer quite the same level of high-end testing as 3DMark does, but it's good to use in conjunction with other software to get a more complete benchmark test.

With a good deal of post-processing effects powering the visuals of *The Witcher 3*, it's a great option for seeing what your machine can do.

Games to test with

Battlefield V

DICE are reputed for creating one of the best game engines in the industry, to such a point that its Frostbite engine is pretty much exclusively used across all of Electronic Arts' major releases. BFV is a beast that comes with numerous post-processing effects to help make the digital worlds that DICE has one of the most impressive, yet.

The Witcher 3: Wild Hunt

As much as this game is a visual feast – what with all its colour and post-processing effects – the real benefit in using it to test your graphics card is its implementation of HDR (high-dynamic range) rendering. It isn't exclusively used in *The Witcher 3*, but it is the core reason that the game looks as bright and vibrant as it does. Plus, it's a pretty good RPG too.

Assassin's Creed Odyssey

Any open-world game can be taxing on a gaming machine, and historically the *Assassin's Creed* hasn't always earned itself top marks. However, with its Grecian instalment, Ubisoft has put considerable effort into making it the most impressive yet. With huge draw distances, large and clear textures and amazing lighting systems, *Odyssey* is certainly one to consider for putting your PC through its paces.

Forza Horizon 4

Racing games have a heritage of pushing the graphical envelope somewhat, and the *Forza* series is especially reputed for that. *Forza Horizon 4* is the latest in the series and has an open world to explore, which adds to the technical tax that it puts on your machine. The fact that it's a solidly entertaining racing game only helps to make it more tempting.

Metro Exodus

The *Metro* series didn't really step up its visual appearance until the more recent releases, and *Metro Exodus* is perhaps the more visually impressive from the developer. Sure, its models and textures might not be the most outstanding up close, but with a number of fancy design choices – like realistic fog, frost and condensation – and a very immediate first-person viewpoint, there's a lot that goes on under the hood here.

Grand Theft Auto V

Though it's a few years old now, *GTA V* is just as popular as it was when it was first released. The mix of huge open-world gameplay and multiplayer madness has kept it relevant, and graphically it looks a treat, too. There are always mods and extras to enhance certain aspects of the visuals, if you really fancy it.

First-person shooters are often the best choices for seeing what your machine can do, but *Metro Exodus* is particularly good for that.

Grand Theft Auto has always been a leader when it comes to open world gameplay, but the PC version of GTA V benefits from considerably better graphics than the console versions.

7

PART 7 Maintenance and settings

Even if you built your brand new gaming PC yourself, just like any piece of hardware it will fall victim to the tests of time. What this means is that your components will age and eventually – hopefully many years down the line – they will finally give up the ghost. Mercifully there are things you can do to help maintain your new PC, and it's highly recommended you do.

There are many ways you can keep your PC running as well as the day it was put together, whether it's clearing away the layers of dust from your PC's parts or making sure your hard drive is free of clutter and unwanted files. There are things you can alter in the settings of your games, too, that will allow you to make the most of your hardware, even when it is beginning to age beyond advancements in computing technology. There's an art to maintaining a PC and it does require a bit of willpower; none of this will be fun to do, but if you set aside just an hour or so a month to keep on top of potential problems then you'll be able to keep your PC fit and healthy for much longer. And, of course, eventually a time will come when you'll need to look for upgrades to your machine to help keep your gaming as high fidelity as possible. Luckily this section will help you through all that.

PART 7 Maintaining your hardware

When it comes to maintenance of your PC hardware there are, thankfully, only a couple of things you need to do. Frankly, providing everything's installed properly, there are no reasons why your hardware should have shifted at all. If you move your PC regularly the wires might need poking back into out-of-the way places, but besides that the hardware you install doesn't need much special treatment.

With that said, however, there is one major threat: dust. It's an unavoidable problem, sadly, and one that requires a great deal of effort in ensuring the build-up isn't ever too much. Dust will increase the temperature that your parts run at, with your cooling fans struggling to move cool air around as effectively and hardware such as your graphics card insulating itself – thus running hotter the longer it is under load. You can use the following steps as often as you think necessary, but we'd recommend a poke around your machine perhaps once a month to keep an eye on any dust build-up, but leave it no more than six months. Any longer than that and the dust will become harder and harder to clean off.

Then there is the thermal paste on your CPU, a process that can be quite intimidating for first-timers. If you find your CPU is becoming incredibly hot and perhaps even dramatically affecting the stability of your PC then it might be time to clean up the thermal paste between your air cooler and the CPU chip. Some recommend replacing the thermal paste about once a year – and there are benefits to that – but providing you're not overclocking your machine you should be okay to leave the stock paste on there for a couple of years at least.

Necessary equipment

Compressed air
A can of compressed air is easily bought from any hardware store and is the safest, most efficient way of cleaning dust off computer parts. Only use short bursts when using compressed air, since longer blasts could result in condensation. Alternatively you can use a powered air blower, which functions in the same way.

Static-free cloth
These special cloths are safe to use on computer parts since they won't fry your hardware with any accidental static electricity. You won't want to use this to clean every part of your machine but it can give you a more effective means of removal on flat surfaces – such as the casing on graphics cards – that can become more heavily caked in dust. Absolutely do not attempt to clean any part of your PC with a cloth if it isn't static-free.

Vacuum
You won't want to use a full-powered vacuum on the inside of your PC – the static and power involved would be incredibly damaging for your PC. However, using the nozzle will be important for cleaning up all that dust later on, and if you can get a weaker hand-vacuum you'll find it's great for gathering that pesky dust.

Cleaning away dust
- Start by unplugging all the cables from your PC, and place it on a flat surface – standing is fine in this case, since dust will simply fall back on to the motherboard if it is lying flat. Remove any side panels you have, both if your case has two.
- At this point take note of any cables. Though they should already be tidied away, it's good to check and make sure they won't cause any accidents with your hardware. If they aren't already, use cable ties to tidy away any loose cables.
- Using a can of compressed air, blow on each of the parts to dislodge any dust. Do this at an angle but fairly close so as to ensure the dust flies out away from the case. Pay particular attention to each of your PC's fans, the power supply unit

You can buy cans of compressed air for next to nothing at practically any hardware store. It's great for cleaning in between keyboard keys too.

(this is imperative) and any extra cards installed into the PCI slots – such as your graphics card.

■ If you haven't much space in your case you can consider removing the power supply unit and its connected cables. This will free up a large chunk of space to get a better angle, and will make it easier to clear away any dust from parts blocked by the cables themselves. Remember to wipe the cables clean too using the static-free cloth.

■ The motherboard itself should be relatively free of dust – providing it is positioned upright, as is the situation for most cases. All the same, give it a spray across the whole motherboard from about three or four inches away to knock off any dust.

■ If you have a smaller nozzle to attach, do so and use that to blow away any dust in between the small crevices – such as between the memory bays or around the CPU area. Make sure you're thorough with this nozzle, since it will focus the air a lot more intensely.

■ Finally use your static-free cloth for very gentle strokes across flat surfaces and hard edges, such as the top of your graphics card, storage drives or the edges of your RAM and fans. The base of the case, now, will likely need dusting too, and if you removed the PSU it'll be easier to clean. Be gentle here, only use a small portion of the cloth at a time and don't use this to clean the motherboard or chips on parts like the graphics card; the cloth could easily get snagged on something and cause damage.

Replacing thermal paste

■ If you find your CPU becoming unreasonably hot during use, it might be time to consider replacing the thermal paste between your CPU chip and the motherboard. Some recommend replacing this paste once every 12 months, but if you're inexperienced it's better to leave well alone until you find problems with your CPU unexpectedly affecting performance.

■ You'll need to remove any fans installed on to the CPU, whether that is the stock fan that comes with the chip or any aftermarket installation you've opted for. Leave the CPU installed, but first you'll want to clean the heatsink on the fan.

■ Clean away the existing thermal paste on the heatsink. Use a flat edge, such as an old credit card or a business card, to wipe the majority of the paste away and then use isopropyl alcohol and a cloth to wipe away the remaining paste. Make sure all of the paste has been removed.

■ Now repeat the process for the CPU, again making sure you keep it installed in the motherboard. Use isopropyl alcohol to ensure the CPU is completely free of old thermal paste.

■ Now apply new thermal paste, which can be bought in most hardware stores or online very easily. Squeeze roughly a pea-sized amount of thermal paste on to the centre of the CPU and then place and reattach the heatsink squarely on top to spread the paste evenly across the back of the chip. Don't try to spread it yourself, since it needs to remain even.

■ Some thermal pastes require specific methods of application, so simply refer to the instructions with your product to ensure you apply it correctly.

Thermal paste comes in all shapes and sizes, but it's not too complicated. The Arctic range is generally the most popular.

PART

Maintaining the software

It's somewhat ironic that physically cleaning your PC is much less tiresome than doing so digitally. Through natural use of your computer it will, inevitably, become a little untidy. Whether you use it primarily for gaming or not, your PC's software will become filled with redundant programs, duplicate files and folders and even leftover temporary installation files. It's an inevitability, really, and all this excess can slow your PC down, not dramatically at first but if you don't keep the spring cleaning up you'll find it will eventually have a noticeable effect on your PC's performance.

What you need to do, then, is make a point of cleaning up your software whenever you can. It doesn't have to be a strict, regular thing but you may find it becomes something of a habit to follow these few steps once a month or so, and in doing so you'll make sure your PC never becomes bogged down with data. It could be worth taking this time to also back up any important data or files you might have

installed on your hard drive; as sad as it is to say, hard drive failures can happen to even the most organised of PC users. Follow these few tips every so often, however, and your PC will remain as streamlined as the day you made it.

Uninstall unwanted software

Whether it's games you no longer play, patchers you no longer need or even general PC programs

If you're never going to play a game again, you may as well uninstall it – even if the space it takes up is inconsequential.

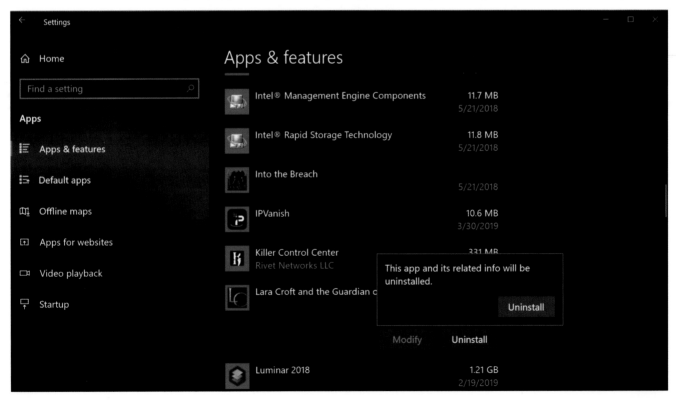

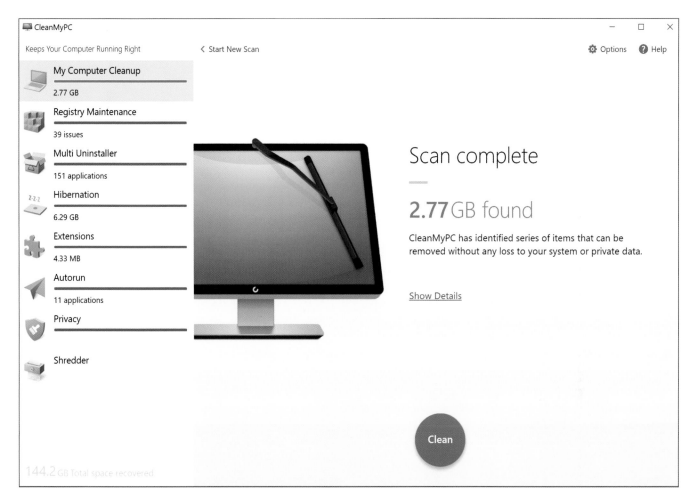

you downloaded but found you never really needed, there are always programs lying around installed on your hard drive that you might not really have much use for. Head into the operating system's software removal feature – in Windows it is termed 'Add or Remove programs' or 'Programs and Features' in the control panel – and scroll through the list of options. While it is beneficial to search by size, if you're doing a spot of cleaning it might be better to search alphabetically, where you can take a better look at the programs themselves. Any you don't use – or use very rarely – can be uninstalled, freeing up space and removing any would-be memory usage. Remember you can always locate the folder where the program's files are installed and look for an executable that will remove the files for you.

Use a storage cleaning software

It might seem somewhat counterproductive to download software to clean up your software, but there are some that help greatly in the battle against messy machines. Some you will have to pay for, while others – like CCleaner – are available almost entirely for free for a wide number of your software maintenance needs. The real benefit of these tools are their 'Cleaner' options, where you can easily – in one menu – remove any unwanted, temporary or duplicate files. It's great for ease of use, and can even let you check the files you want cleaned away and the files you don't. There are many other programs out there that will claim to 'enhance the performance of your PC', but in truth some of them are little more than glorified software removal programs or perhaps even malware. Stick with something you can see is reliable – such as CleanMyPC or CCleaner – which are popular for a reason and will do everything you need.

Clear caches, download folder and desktop

While CCleaner can help with many of these functions, it's worth drawing attention to the importance of it. Temporary files and cached data is the biggest threat to PC performance because it is information that is quite regularly referenced and re-referenced by software that you use often – in particular your internet

It's good to go through defragmentation every so often, if only so it keeps your hard drive running as smoothly as possible.

browser – even if that data is old and no longer needed. Clearing out your history, cached files and temporary files will improve performance since there won't be quite as much information that your CPU and memory needs to take note of. Again, CCleaner is great for helping with this. Outside of that it's worth checking any folders that might naturally accrue files that eventually become old and irrelevant, such as your Downloads, Documents and Pictures folders. Find these folders and go through the files inside to delete those you don't need. Repeat the process for your desktop, which can – for many – become something of a dumping ground for shortcuts and downloaded files. And

don't forget to clear your recycling bin out once you've done all this.

Go through defragmentation

Hard drives – by their very nature – can become a little confused. With so much data writing and rewriting going on in even a single session on your PC, months of use can cause your files to become fragmented, slowing your PC down as it has to search for information in a wider number of places. It's a healthy process to go through defragmentation – called disk optimisation on Windows 10 – to analyse your hard drives and recalibrate the data so it can be more easily found. There are a number of software options

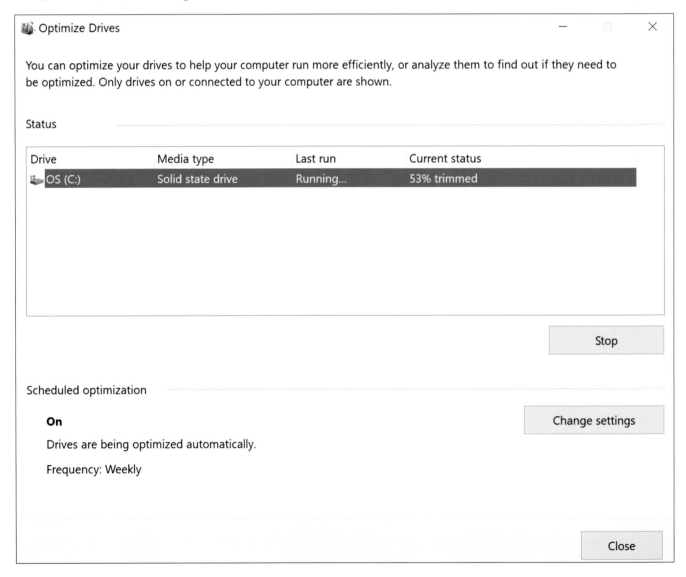

out there that help with defragmentation, but if you're running Windows you'll likely find that the basic tool pre-installed on to your system will be more than enough to proceed with this step. Either way it's good to defragment your hard drive perhaps three or four times a year.

Cancel launch start-up programs

Having numerous programs that boot up at the same time as your operating system can slow down your PC; you've likely used an old PC before that needs a few minutes to 'settle' before it can be properly used – that's the resultant effect of the menace of start-up software. Some you will want booting up alongside your PC – such as antivirus software – but in truth there are many times where it can be better to cancel many of the programs that do start up on launch. Again, there is software that can help with this but if you don't fancy using such programs, then you can do it yourself with Windows. Open up Task Manager (type it into the Start Menu if you don't know how to find it) and then select the 'Startup' tab. Here you'll see all the programs that are attempting to boot up alongside Windows, simply disable the ones you don't need (or don't want to start up until you need them) and the job is done.

After a year or two, you may be surprised to find so many programs starting up alongside Windows. You won't need all of them.

Task Manager

File Options View

Processes Performance App history **Startup** Users Details Services

Last BIOS time: **10.8 seconds**

Name	Publisher	Status	Startup impact
> Delayed launcher	Intel Corporation	Enabled	High
HD Audio Background Proc...	Realtek Semiconductor	Enabled	Low
HD Audio Background Proc...	Realtek Semiconductor	Enabled	Low
Killer Control Center	Rivet Networks LLC	Disabled	None
> Mailbird	Mailbird	Enabled	High
Microsoft OneDrive	Microsoft Corporation	Disabled	None
Realtek HD Audio Manager	Realtek Semiconductor	Enabled	Medium
Sophos Home User Interface	Sophos Limited	Enabled	Medium
> Sticky Password	Lamantine Software a.s.	Enabled	High
Waves MaxxAudio Service A...	Waves Audio Ltd.	Enabled	High
Windows Defender notificat...	Microsoft Corporation	Enabled	Medium
XBoxStat.exe	Microsoft Corporation	Enabled	Low

⌃ Fewer details

Disable

PART

Upgrading existing parts

There's no avoiding the onset of age, and technology is no different. When it comes to your PC, the amount of time it can survive before it becomes obsolete is entirely dependent on the initial build. If you've spent over £1,000 to make sure your PC is a top-of-the-line piece of kit then you can be sure that – barring any unexpected faults with any given part – it'll last you a good few years running games at their very best. Eventually it will come to a point when enough is enough, however, and you may not want to simply start all over again. That would be costly, more than anything else.

At this point you'll need to figure out what hardware it is you need to replace – and in all likelihood it'll be the graphics card first – and then you'll need to figure out what it is you can upgrade it with. This follows the same sorts of stipulations that you would've had when originally buying the hardware, which is to say ensuring they match certain criteria with the motherboard, case and other compatible parts. Providing you fulfil these criteria you'll be okay to upgrade whichever part you want, following the same procedures listed in the 'Build a gaming PC' section. We don't need to cover that again since the process is the same (except you're removing the existing part first), so instead we'll explain how to know which part to upgrade, and what to upgrade it with.

Your system memory is the quickest, easiest and cheapest upgrade you can go for – but make sure you only buy RAM with the same channel setup as your motherboard.

When to upgrade your graphics card

For PC gamers the most integral part of their gaming experience is the graphics card. This is the piece of hardware that creates the visuals for your games, and if that is not able to perform as well as it used to it will leave your games stuttering under the weight of their graphical prowess. At what point you deem it important to upgrade your GPU comes down to entirely what standard you want to play your games at. You can gradually lower the

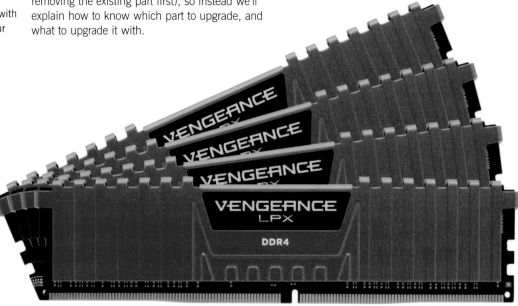

Because of the standardised nature of PC hardware these days it's often very simple upgrading different parts, even the likes of GPUs. Make sure the upgrades are compatible, however.

settings in-game, for example, to extend the life of the GPU by playing games with inferior graphical options activated. It means you won't be able to enjoy games at their absolute best, but you'll get a good few months out of the card itself. Once it becomes a struggle to find a balance between a visual fidelity you're happy with and a consistent, stable frame rate then you know it's time to upgrade. Frame rate is the most important aspect, since making sure that is steady allows for a more enjoyable experience. With regards to what you should upgrade with, well that comes largely down to what is considered to be the 'best' at the time. Thankfully GPUs tend to follow a fairly familiar pattern, so if you spent £300 on a card initially then look to spend the same the second time around – you'll roughly get something in the same ballpark, in terms of comparative power – that you had previously.

When to upgrade your memory

RAM is often the easiest upgrade to go for. If you find your machine is taking a while to load or struggling when multitasking programs – such as switching between a fullscreen game and the Steam program – then it's often easier to upgrade your RAM rather than anything else. It's only a temporary fix since there are far more important parts – at least when it comes to the speed of your computer – than the memory, but it's also a fairly low-cost upgrade too. You'll likely be looking at a cost of around £100 to upgrade your memory rather than

the £300–400 for any other more significant piece of hardware, so it's an easy switch. Just make sure that if you do upgrade your RAM, do so with the exact same memory as before (if you're adding to it) or, preferably, a completely new set. Be sure to follow our tips on buying memory at the front of the book to know how best to proceed when buying RAM.

When to upgrade your CPU

It's tougher to detect when a CPU is holding back your gaming performance, especially since modern games often rely more heavily on your graphics card's capabilities. Finding out which part is causing the bottleneck is difficult, but since the CPU handles logical computation then testing it out with the latest strategy game (or anything with a lot of complex AI, really) will help; if it takes much longer than it should then, chances are, it's your CPU. However, you don't want to shell out another £300 for a 'chance' that your CPU is the problem; in this case download and install HWMonitor, a piece of software that will calculate a percentage of your hardware's capacities and how close it is to its maximum. When upgrading, however, you need to be very certain that the CPU you're buying has the same socket as your motherboard, and in all likelihood you'll need to buy a new motherboard too. If your PC is older than two years, then you'll probably need to upgrade the motherboard, so be sure to check out the compatibility.

When to upgrade your storage

This is probably the only upgrade situation that is guided more by your own personal preference

Cooling options are important for the longevity of your PC, but if you're considering overclocking you should also make sure your PC's temperature will stay down.

than technical limits. If you find your hard drive is getting full and you're having to regularly juggle installed games, then it might be time to upgrade your storage. The beauty of upgrading your hard drive, however, is the fact that you have numerous options. You can combine a second hard drive alongside your older one to run two storages drives, with one acting as a sort of dumping ground. Alternatively you could swap it out entirely for a much larger equivalent, and use the older hard drive as a backup storage drive (you can actually buy cases to turn an existing drive into a portable storage drive). Or you might decide to splash out for a quicker, more efficient solid state drive (SSD), which by the time you need to upgrade will have reduced even more in price with much larger capacities available. Remember, however, that though your hard drive might seem sufficient for now, the older a HDD gets the more likely it is to fail – for the safety of all your stored data it can often be better to pre-empt any failure if your drive is three or four years old.

When to upgrade your cooling

Providing you've not had any temperature problems with your system since its installation

– and truth be told, there's no reason why you ought to – then the only reason you might need to upgrade your current cooling system is when you make a change to the hardware in your PC. This could be swapping a GPU out for a much more powerful and power-hungry equivalent, for example, or maybe you've been tempted by our guide on overclocking. In either case, if you're increasing the overall power consumption of your machine then you may also be increasing the running temperature, and at this point the cooling system you have might not be adequate. Use software to check the running temperature of your various parts when under strain to check this is the case, though – if something is getting too hot, it will likely be noticeable in performance drops anyway. When upgrading you'll need to think about what options are open to you. Once upon a time people would cut holes into side panels and install secondary or tertiary fans, but these days a single upgrade to the existing fan should be enough. If not, then consider water cooling as your last option before ultimately resorting to underclocking (or resetting) the running capabilities of your CPU, GPU or memory.

PART

In-game settings explained

PC gaming is replete with often hundreds of little settings and tweaks that can be made to a game to make it run optimally on your machine. Since every PC is different – from the hardware installed to the active, running software – it's impossible for developers to create games that can run exactly the same across all forms of PC hardware. It works on consoles because the hardware is always the same, it's predictable; on PCs more work needs to be done to enable as wide a range of users as possible. That's where the visual settings come in, letting you tweak a game's options to make it run as smoothly as possible with as high a fidelity as possible on whatever tier of build your PC is.

Here's an example of screen tearing, an often unavoidable problem that can be resolved by enabling VSync.

Now if you'd rather not get into the nitty-gritty of tailoring settings for your needs then more often than not there is a set of options to pick from, usually with 'Ultra' at the top end and 'Low' at the bottom. These are sets of generic changes to the settings, and will suffice for those who can't be bothered tinkering with the settings. However, there's also a wide range of options and though the ones that are available differ from game to game, their meanings never change. There is a

lot of jargon involved here, so we're going to bust that wide open and explain a little bit about what it is these different settings change and why they are important. Remember: not all of these will be in every game, and there may well be some game-specific options too – such as character model quality. Use your own judgement in this regard, but note that post-processing effects often have a greater impact on your processing than high polygon counts.

Type of setting	What it affects	Details
Resolution	The number of pixels – and therefore clarity of the image – that is rendered onto your monitor.	Resolution is important for the visual fidelity, and ideally you'll render a game to match that of your monitor's resolution (probably 1080p or 1440p). However, it is also possible to render higher than your monitor's resolution, which will be downscaled to fit the screen and provide even greater detail.
VSync	Locks the frame rate to either 30 or 60 frames per second.	Some games struggle rendering fast moving actions – such as camera control – and this can result in screen-tearing. Enabling Vertical Synchronisation prevents any erratic frame-rate fluctuations to eliminate this.
Adaptive VSync	The same as VSync, but disables itself when dropping below 60 frames per second.	With VSync, if a frame rate drops below 60FPS it will then switch to 30FPS – but if this happens often it can cause stuttering. NVIDIA's Adaptive VSync stops this by switching VSync off if the frame rate drops below 60FPS.
View distance	Controls the distance that is rendered.	This might be obvious, but by controlling the distance at which the game world is rendered you can better control your PC's performance. The game world is not completely rendered, and is instead only rendered when it comes into view – this option controls the distance that occurs at.
Field of view	Controls the 'wideness' of your character's view.	Popular in first-person games, field of view lets you alter the angle at which the camera – or your character – is able to see. On wider monitors this can create a much more realistic viewpoint, and give you a greater vision while playing. Useful for multiplayer games.
GSync/Freesync	With a compatible monitor this can alter the screen's refresh rate to match the frame rate.	As relatively new technology (NVIDIA has GSync, AMD has Freesync) there aren't all that many cases where this is possible, but if you have a compatible GPU and monitor, it will remove any screen tearing and input lag issues with VSync.
Texture quality	Controls the resolution of in-game textures.	Though not always, you can sometimes control the quality of textures – naturally improving performance if opting for lower-quality textures.
Bilinear/Trilinear Filtering	Affects the way 2D images – or textures – are displayed on a 3D model from different angles.	Filtering helps keep control of the way textures work on 3D models, and bilinear is the most basic method of this. Trilinear is better, but only in that it takes samples from nearby textures too.
Anisotropic Filtering	Affects the way 2D images – or textures – are displayed on a 3D model from different angles.	This is a stronger form of filtering that takes into account many more factors. It requires more processing power, of course, but enables greater clarity at further ranges. Better for avoiding blurriness of textures at longer distances.
Anti-aliasing (MSAA – Multisampling)	Smooths hard edges of pixels for a more natural appearance.	MSAA – or multisampling anti-aliasing – is the basic form of AA for videogames, offering decent results with good efficiency. For any anti-aliasing, the higher number before this means more accuracy at a higher cost on your CPU and GPU.
Anti-aliasing (CSAA – Coverage sampling)	Smooths hard edges of pixels for a more natural appearance.	This is NVIDIA's version of MSAA, and provides the same results with greater efficiency. For any anti-aliasing, the higher number before this means more accuracy at a higher cost on your CPU and GPU.
Anti-aliasing (CFAA – Custom filter)	Smooths hard edges of pixels for a more natural appearance.	This is AMD's version of MSAA, a more efficient version of the aliasing with similar results. For any anti-aliasing, the higher number before this means more accuracy at a higher cost on your CPU and GPU.
Anti-aliasing (FXAA – Fast approximate)	Smooths hard edges of pixels for a more natural appearance.	As the name suggests, this anti-aliasing is a quick-action version. Rather than analyse different models, FXAA instead applies a post-processing filter to smooth the entire scene. For any anti-aliasing, the higher number before this means more accuracy at a higher cost on your CPU and GPU.

Type of setting	What it affects	Details
Anti-aliasing (MLAA – Morphological)	Smooths hard edges of pixels for a more natural appearance.	A form of AA unique to AMD cards. This uses a unique algorithm to detect jagged edges in an entire frame/scene, and smooths it out. For any anti-aliasing, the higher number before this means more accuracy at a higher cost on your CPU and GPU.
Anti-aliasing (SMAA – Enhanced Subpixel Morphological)	Smooths hard edges of pixels for a more natural appearance.	An enhanced version of MLAA that also utilises methods of MSAA. For any anti-aliasing, the higher number before this means more accuracy at a higher cost on your CPU and GPU.
Anti-aliasing (TXAA – Temporal)	Smooths hard edges of pixels for a more natural appearance.	Utilises MSAA techniques with other filters, while using existing frame AA data to compute the next frame. For any anti-aliasing, the higher number before this meansmore accuracy at a higher cost on your CPU and GPU.
Anti-aliasing (MFAA – Multi-frame)	Smooths hard edges of pixels for a more natural appearance.	Exclusively to NVIDIA's new Maxwell range, MFAA allows more customisable patterns of anti-aliasing. For any anti-aliasing, the higher number before this means more accuracy at a higher cost on your CPU and GPU.
Ambient occlusion (SSAO)	Attempts to display lighting in a more realistic fashion.	As a process-heavy option, SSAO can be one of the first you can disable. It can help to make lighting look more realistic since it attempts to calculate which parts of a scene should have less light than another.
Bloom	Exaggerates lighting for a stronger visual appearance.	Bloom is more of an artistic element, and is most notable for having the light render more intensely, appearing to spill out over the edges of windows and the like. Sometimes it helps create a unique visual cue, but can often be disabled.
Depth of field	Visual effect to make distant or peripheral vision blurred.	Depth of field is a post-processing effect that draws attention to centralised objects while additional details appear blurred. As a post-processing effect, this is often superfluous and can be disabled.
Detail quality	Controls the quality of particular details.	This can often take any form, sometimes simply called 'Detail' and other times with greater specificity, such as 'Grass/Foliage detail'. This is often referring to more minute elements of a game, however, and can be one of the first adjustments you need to make.
HDR (High dymanic range) lighting	Improves the range of detail from light areas to darkened areas.	HDR is a very process-heavy feature that can be disabled first if your PC is beginning to age. A higher range allows for better detail in the darkest and lightest parts of a scene.
Shadow quality	Controls the overall quality of shadows.	As a superfluous graphical option, shadows can often be controlled – as with textures – to better match your hardware. Lower quality provides better performance.
Motion blur	Adds blurring to camera movements.	For a more cinematic feel, this post-processing effect replicates the way a camera processes movement – namely blurring pixels to give the impression of speed or movement.
Particle effects	Controls the strength, quality or regularity of particle effects.	Particle effects are often superfluous extras that help make a scene feel more realistic, such as dust mites floating in a beam of light or dirt being kicked up off the ground during a fight. Some games give you the option to customise these elements in a number of ways.
PhysX	Adds more realistic physics-based actions.	PhysX controls a game's ability to render realistic physics-based reactions – such as debris flying away after a devastating blow. It is often a toggleable option.

PART  **Testing and fault-finding**

So your new PC is dead. You've finished the build, closed the case, patted yourself on the back, turned on the power and … nothing. Not a peep.

This is a terrible moment in anyone's life and it is entirely natural to feel that heart-wrenching sinking feeling. We're here to help you solve your problems, but first let's lay down a couple of pointers. These aren't exactly rules or directions, but do please think of them as well-intentioned advice.

The first point is not to panic. Second, if in doubt wait it out. If you're British, stop and make a cup of tea. You may well have a problem or even a number of problems, but you don't want to make things worse, so take a step back and have a nice cup of tea (other beverages are available). Third, take nothing for granted. Make no assumptions. Always return to first principles. That sounds like three points, but it is actually the same thing said three ways. One of the fatal mistakes when you are fault-finding is to say: 'I have confirmed that part A works and that part B works so it follows that part C is faulty.' You need to be scientific. The truly cautious person will say: 'I think I have confirmed that part A works and it appears that part B works so it follows that part C is possibly faulty.' Fourth, avoid tunnel vision and keep your eyes wide open. The following tale may be just that, but it happens. Many years ago, back when we had telephones with a dial in the middle, an office worker phoned an IT support line: 'Hello, my computer is dead.'

The support guy walked through their script and asked the office person to check a few things. 'Can you look round the back of the computer and check the VGA cable is secure at both the PC and the monitor.'

'No I cannot do that,' came the reply, 'I can't see anything as the power cut has taken out the lights.'

PART  **Troubleshooting**

Let's assume you've built your PC, turned it on for the first time ... and nothing happens. You can't get into BIOS, let alone install Windows. How and where do you begin to troubleshoot?

In fact, identifying a problem at this stage is very much easier than down the road when you've got a printer, scanner, webcam and goodness knows what other hardware attached; not to mention 57 software programs doing their utmost to interfere with one another, a real risk of viruses and perhaps a utility suite that does more harm than good. Your computer will never be so easy to diagnose and cure as it is right now.

Check the cables

The very first step is all too obvious but all too often overlooked: check that all external cables are securely connected in the correct places:

- The computer's PSU should be plugged into a mains wall socket (or power gangplank).
- So should the monitor.
- The mains electricity supply should be turned on at the wall.
- The monitor should be connected to the video card's VGA, DVI or HDMI output.
- The keyboard should be connected to the computer's PS/2-style keyboard port (not to a USB port, unless USB support has already been enabled in BIOS, and not to the mouse port).
- The PSU should be set to the correct voltage and turned on.

Now turn on the monitor. A power indication LED on the monitor housing should illuminate and, hopefully, you'll see something on the screen. If not, re-read the monitor manual and double-check that you've correctly identified the on/off switch and are not busy fiddling with the brightness or contrast controls. It's not always obvious which switch is which. If the power light still does not come on, it sounds like the monitor itself may be at fault. Try changing the fuse in the cable. Ideally, test the monitor with another PC.

Internal inspection

Now turn on the PC itself. Press the large on/off switch on the front of the case, not the smaller reset switch. You should hear the whirring of internal fans and either a single beep or a sequence of beeps. But let's assume that all seems lifeless. Again, check/change the fuse in the PSU power cable. If this doesn't help, unplug all cables, including the monitor, take off the case covers and lay the computer on its side. Now systematically check every internal connection. Again, here's a quick checklist to tick off:

- The PSU should be connected to the motherboard with a large 24-pin plug and also, if appropriate, with ATX 12V and ATX Auxiliary cables.
- The heatsink fan should be plugged into a power socket on the motherboard.
- The case fans should be likewise connected.
- All drives should be connected to the appropriate sockets on the motherboard with ribbon cables.
- All drives should be connected to the PSU with power cables.
- The graphics card should be securely sited in its AGP or PCI Express slot.
- All other expansion cards should be likewise in place.
- Look for loose screws inside the case, lest one should be causing a short circuit.
- Check the front panel connections. If the case's on/off switch is disconnected from the motherboard, you won't be able to start the system.
- Are any cables snagging on fans?
- Are the retention clips on the memory DIMMs fully closed?
- Does anything on the motherboard look obviously broken or damaged?

The modular design of modern PSUs is superb but adds a load of extra connections that can cause problems.

Disconnect each cable in turn and look for bent pins on the plugs and sockets. These can usually be straightened with small, pointy pliers and a steady hand. Reconnect everything, including the monitor and power cable, and turn the computer on once more. Leave the covers off to aid observation. Does it now burst into life as if by magic? Rather gallingly, unplugging and replacing a cable is sometimes all it takes to fix an elusive but strictly temporary glitch.

PSU problems

Look for an LED on the motherboard (check the manual for its location). This should illuminate whenever the PSU is connected to the mains power and turned on, even when the computer itself is off. The LED confirms that the motherboard is receiving power; if it stays dark, the PSU itself may be at fault.

When you turn on the computer, do the fans remain static? Does the CD drive disc tray refuse to open? Is all depressingly dead? This would confirm the PSU as the problem. Use an alternative power cable, perhaps borrowed from the monitor, just to be sure. If still nothing happens, remove and replace the PSU.

NEVER TRY TO OPEN OR REPAIR A PSU. Nor should you try running it while it's disconnected from the motherboard, as a PSU can only operate with a load.

Finding a connection fault

By now you should be reasonably confident that you have mains power arriving at the input of your PSU. Until a few years ago, the fact that mains power arrived at the PSU pretty much

guaranteed that 12V, 5V and 3.3V would flow to the motherboard, graphics card and SSD, and if it didn't then you could be confident the PSU was faulty.

The rise of the modular PSU changed all that. While the modular PSU with its detachable cables looks much neater than the messy old PSUs from the past, this change introduces a load of new connection points.

The simple rule of thumb is that if a plug fits in a socket you are safe to use it, but it makes sense to read the legends printed on the cables and PSU just to make sure you have the right thing in the right place. There is a good chance that the cables will all appear to be properly connected, but you need to be sure you hear that satisfying click as you push them into place. If you have any doubts, give each cable a gentle tug to ensure it is secure.

No doubt you have carefully routed the PSU cables inside your PC so that they feed around the back of the motherboard tray and, inevitably, make some twists and turns en route to their destination. If you have any doubt in your mind, it is best to make direct connections and simply feed the cables across the motherboard. You can always tidy it up once you have fixed your problems, but for the moment you simply need power and, of course, to ensure the cables are clear of any fans.

Power supply to your graphics card is a slightly vexing issue. You don't need much power to start Windows running and get the desktop displayed on your monitor, but every graphics card on the market insists that you connect those dratted 6-pin and 8-pin connectors before the system will even think

If you haven't got enough power heading to your graphics card(s), you can expect to hit problems.

This EVGA Z87 Stinger is a prime example of a motherboard that sports a number of premium features such as micro buttons and a debug display.

of starting. Ideally, if you are using a CPU or APU that contains a graphics core, you would temporarily remove your graphics card(s) to take them out of the equation.

Power On Self Test (POST)

The photo of this EVGA Z87 Stinger Mini-ITX motherboard (opposite) shows three things of interest. At the bottom right we have the front panel header connections, at the top right there is the POST debug display and at the top there are Power and Reset buttons. These are premium features that you won't find on mainstream and budget motherboards, but hopefully you have aimed high with your gaming PC build. The colour-coded front panel headers make life much easier when you connect the Power and Reset buttons along with the Power and Activity LEDs. These connections are all interchangeable and it is alarmingly easy to plug things together incorrectly or even to miss the header and only engage with one pin rather than two. If you make that mistake, you can press the Power button all you like and your perfectly functioning PC will refuse to respond. The same thing applies if the wiring to the front of the case is damaged or the button is faulty.

Using the Power micro buttons bypasses this problem entirely. If you don't have micro buttons on your motherboard, the time-honoured alternative is to use a plain screwdriver to short the two header pins. Under no circumstances short the pins with a jumper to make a permanent connection – this is a momentary connection that sends a signal to the PSU to get things started. As you probably know, if you press and hold the Power button for ten seconds when your PC is running you will actually force it to shut down.

The other advantage of a premium motherboard is the POST code debug display. During POST (Power On Self Test) the display shows a series of two character codes that you can interpret to see the progress of your system start-up. We've posted the most popular codes later in this section.

With a premium motherboard you can tell in moments whether or not you have power and whether the power button is attempting to boot your new PC into life. With a lesser motherboard you are pretty much in the dark between the time the fans start turning and when the reassuring Windows logo appears on your screen.

PART  Finding faulty hardware

If you still have a dead PC then the time has come to search for faulty hardware. Sadly if you've made sure every piece of hardware is properly installed, there are no faults with your power supply and that the PSU is correctly connected to every necessary part, well ... that means you've got a faulty piece of hardware somewhere. It could be as simple as a mistake in the installation, though, so don't despair too much.

Installing your new hardware in a case can introduce all sorts of unexpected problems, even if you use high-end hardware such as this Phanteks Enthoo Pro.

If you have previously run the hardware you will have hopefully tracked down the installation problem by the simple procedure of retracing your steps. If you haven't and you are utterly stumped then pull the motherboard assembly from the case and give it a try. It is so much quicker and easier to check components when you have good access and a PC case can be a tough working environment. Check each of the following processes one by one to try and locate your issue.

- The most obvious candidate is the CPU socket on your Intel motherboard as the CPU is effectively flat and sits on a series of 1,150 tiny springs that make contact. The CPU package has a couple of notches that engage with the socket on the motherboard and provided you carefully rest it in place then all is well. It only takes a tiny slip and you can drop the CPU on to the motherboard, which can end up causing all sorts of damage. You then have to make a decision about returning the motherboard, attempting to fix the damage or buying a replacement.
- AMD customers are in a slightly different position as AMD uses the traditional approach where the CPU carries the pins while the socket is on the motherboard. You are most unlikely to damage the motherboard when you insert the CPU, but it is quite easy

to bend a number of pins unless you line up the CPU quite precisely.
- If you have done something utterly silly such as installing your DDR3 memory the wrong way round then you won't have been able to secure the latches. If you tried something a bit more subtle such as installing DDR2 memory in a DDR3 motherboard (or vice versa) then it either won't fit or the latches won't secure. This hardware has been designed to avoid precisely this problem so if the thing won't go in the slot there is a good reason.
- It is perfectly possible that you have failed to correctly insert a graphics card in its PCI Express slot. You'll feel like an idiot, but we have all done it and the galling thing is that a graphics card can appear to be inserted correctly when it actually requires another push to seat it. Most motherboards have a latch or some sort of locking mechanism to secure the end of the card that sits in the middle of the PC.
- The two snags you need to watch for are the motherboard mounts and the expansion slots in the case. You need to be sure that the motherboard sits flat on its mounts, which are usually a set of metal posts that screw into holes in the side of the case. There is scope in a budget case for these holes to be out of line or for the mounting posts to have some variation, which throws out the alignment of the graphics card.

Damaged components are a nightmare. The question is did you break it or can you claim on the warranty?

Incompatible memory is the stuff of nightmares and can cause endless problems, including an apparently dead PC.

Searching for incompatibility

Having tackled the problems of broken components, loose connections and a lack of power, we move on to the tricky stuff.

Incompatible components can stop you in your tracks or, if you are particularly unfortunate, they can cause problems every once in a while at seemingly random moments. One giveaway is when you press the Power button and the fans rotate slightly in a sort of lurch and then immediately stop. It is obvious the PC is showing signs of life yet clearly it isn't going to burst into action.

PC technology runs on industry standards, which is why you can buy your case, PSU, motherboard, graphics card and cooling system from an array of vendors and have every confidence they will work together. Despite a colossal amount of hard work by the industry, you can run into problems, in particular with your CPU and memory. Your motherboard supports a particular type of processor, but it may well not support every CPU that will fit in the socket. As mentioned in the Anatomy chapter, some AMD AM3+ CPUs require more power than you get from the earlier AM3

socket so if you put the later CPU in an earlier motherboard, it simply won't work.

A more common problem is to find that a motherboard built in, say, September 2014 supports CPUs made up to that point but requires a BIOS update for a CPU that was released in December 2014. You buy motherboard and CPU in January 2015 and find the hardware is incompatible and, humorously, you cannot start the system to update the BIOS. Certain motherboards get round this problem in ingenious ways. Intel offered a number of different methods to update the BIOS on its Intel-branded motherboards including from CD and would allow you to boot into the BIOS to perform the necessary update. Asus has gone a step further with its Republic of Gamers models that support USB BIOS flashback where you can update the BIOS from a flash drive on a bare motherboard that doesn't even have a CPU installed. Let's hope this concept spreads to all manufacturers.

Memory support should be as easy as easy can be. Your motherboard supports DDR3, the CPU memory controller supports DDR3-2,133MHz and you buy some DDR3-

1,600MHz. It is natural to expect the memory would fit and work and while it will only run at 1,600MHz that should be just fine for your needs. Unfortunately you need to refer to your motherboard manufacturer's support site to be certain your chosen memory will work correctly. Some memory will work at reduced speed and other memory will prevent the system from booting. Asus (again) has a neat trick

called MemOK! on certain models that is a compatibility switch. With MemOK! enabled the system will run, and even if the speed is slower than you might like, you can at least confirm that your problem comes down to the memory.

Check your monitor connection

By this stage in the fault-finding game we hope you have a PC that is showing signs of life and the fans are turning. This can lead to the frustrating situation where your new gaming PC appears to be alive and well yet you cannot see anything on the screen.

There was a time when a monitor had a single cable to connect to your PC and that cable was hardwired at one end and had a simple connector at the other. These days you need to select a connection from an array that might include DisplayPort, HDMI, DVI and VGA. Quite a few graphics cards have as many as six outputs.

Once you have decided on the connection you want, plugged it into the graphics card and monitor and ensured the monitor has mains power, you should be ready for action. Turn on the monitor, turn on the PC and wait for the status LED to turn blue (or green, or whatever). Any decent monitor should automatically detect which input is being used so you need to be sure the monitor doesn't have any other inputs in use. However, you might need to use the control buttons to manually select the correct input.

At this stage if you still don't have a picture showing on the monitor, there is something rather obvious that you need to check. These days Intel CPUs include a graphics core and so do certain series of AMD chips and this means you find graphics outputs on the I/O panel of many motherboards. If the BIOS is set to automatically select a graphics output then it shouldn't matter whether you connect to the I/O panel or graphics card, although obviously the integrated graphics will have much lower performance.

The problem comes when the BIOS is set to either use the IGP (Integrated Graphics Processor) or PCI Express output and you connect to the other output, which has been disabled. This will render the PC unusable until you swap from the disabled graphics to the correct set. Once you regain control of your PC you can use the BIOS set-up to enable whichever graphics outputs you want.

Sometimes it can be tricky making the correct connection to your graphics card.

TESTING AND FAULT FINDING

PART 8 Beep and error codes

If it all goes wrong and you still can't get your PC up and running then fear not, because many motherboards have features that can help you decipher precisely what the problem is. These only really occur when the problem is serious enough to prevent it from even booting up, so there aren't often too many to worry about. Here we're reprinting the beep and error codes from AMI and Award, makers of two very commonly used BIOS programs. But worry not if your codes are just a little too complicated to decipher – such as those from Phoenix – because there's always a resource online you can hunt down to discover the solution.

The feared Windows 'Blue Screen of Death' is far less common than it used to be.

```
A problem has been detected and windows has been shut down to prevent damage
to your computer.

DRIVER_IRQL_NOT_LESS_OR_EQUAL

If this is the first time you've seen this Stop error screen,
restart your computer, If this screen appears again, follow
these steps:

Check to make sure any new hardware or software is properly installed.
If this is a new installation, ask your hardware or software manufacturer
for any windows updates you might need.

If problems continue, disable or remove any newly installed hardware
or software. Disable BIOS memory options such as caching or shadowing.
If you need to use Safe Mode to remove or disable components, restart
your computer, press F8 to select Advanced Startup Options, and then
select Safe Mode.

Technical information:

*** STOP: 0x000000D1 (0x0000000C,0x00000002,0x00000000,0xF86B5A89)

***          gv3.sys - Address F86B5A89 base at F86B5000, DateStamp 3dd991eb

Beginning dump of physical memory
Physical memory dump complete.
Contact your system administrator or technical support group for further
assistance.
```

AMI BIOS beep codes

Number of Beeps	Problem	Action
1 short	Memory refresh timer error.	Remove each memory module, clean the connecting edge that plugs into the motherboard socket, and replace. If that doesn't work, try restarting with a single memory module and see if you can identify the culprit by a process of elimination. If you still get the error code, replace with known good modules.
2 short	Parity error.	As with 1 beep above.
3 short	Main memory read/write test error.	As with 1 beep above.
4 short	Motherboard timer not operational.	Either the motherboard is faulty or one of the expansion cards has a problem. Remove all cards except the video card and restart. If the motherboard still issues this beep code, it has a serious, probably fatal problem. If the beeps stop, replace the cards one at a time and restart each time. This should identify the guilty party.
5 short	Processor error.	As with 4 beeps above.
6 short	Keyboard controller BAT test error.	As with 4 beeps above.
7 short	General exception error.	As with 4 beeps above.
8 short	Display memory error.	The video card is missing, faulty or incorrectly installed. Remove, clean the connecting contacts and replace. If that doesn't work, try using a different video card. If you are using integrated video instead of a video card, the motherboard may be faulty.
9 short	ROM checksum error.	As with 4 beeps above.
10 short	CMOS shutdown register read/write error.	As with 4 beeps above.
11 short	Cache memory bad.	As with 4 beeps above.
1 long, 2 short	Failure in video system.	A fault with the video BIOS ROM has occurred. Uninstall the graphics card and use the on-board graphics to find out if your GPU is the one causing the fault.
1 long, 3 short	Memory test failure.	There's an issue with your system memory; reinstall the RAM. If it is still faulty, try running the PC on a single stick of RAM (alternating between different sticks if the fault still occurs).
1 long, 8 short	Display test failure.	A fault with your video card – either your own GPU or on-board graphics on the motherboard – or its memory. The system will boot without it, but it means there's likely a hardware fault with your video card.

AMIBIOS8 Checkpoint and Beep Code List version 1.2. Copyright of American Megatrends, Inc. Reprinted with permission. All rights reserved.

AMI BIOS error codes Here are some examples of onscreen error messages:

Error	Action
Gate20 Error	The BIOS is unable to properly control the motherboard's Gate A20 function, which controls access of memory over 1MB. This may indicate a problem with the motherboard.
Multi-Bit ECC Error	This message will only occur on systems using ECC-enabled memory modules. ECC memory has the ability to correct single-bit errors that may occur from faulty memory modules. A multiple bit corruption of memory has occurred, and the ECC memory algorithm cannot correct it. This may indicate a defective memory module.
Parity Error	Fatal Memory Parity Error. System halts after displaying this message.
Boot Failure	This is a generic message indicating the BIOS could not boot from a particular device. This message is usually followed by other information concerning the device.
Invalid Boot Diskette	A diskette was found in the drive, but it is not configured as a bootable diskette.

AMI BIOS error codes continued:

Error	Action
Drive Not Ready	The BIOS was unable to access the drive because it indicated it was not ready for data transfer. This is often reported by drives when no media is present.
A: Drive Error	The BIOS attempted to configure the A: drive during POST, but was unable to properly configure the device. This may be because of a bad cable or faulty diskette drive.
Insert BOOT diskette in A:	The BIOS attempted to boot from the A: drive, but could not find a proper boot diskette.
Reboot and Select proper Boot device or Insert Boot Media in selected Boot device	BIOS could not find a bootable device in the system and/or removable media drive does not contain media.
NO ROM BASIC	This message occurs on some systems when no bootable device can be detected.
Primary Master Hard Disk Error	The IDE/ATAPI device configured as Primary Master could not be properly initialised by the BIOS. This message is typically displayed when the BIOS is trying to detect and configure IDE/ATAPI devices in POST.
Primary Slave Hard Disk Error	The IDE/ATAPI device configured as Primary Slave could not be properly initialised by the BIOS. This message is typically displayed when the BIOS is trying to detect and configure IDE/ATAPI devices in POST.
Secondary Master Hard Disk Error	The IDE/ATAPI device configured as Secondary Master could not be properly initialised by the BIOS. This message is typically displayed when the BIOS is trying to detect and configure IDE/ATAPI devices in POST.
Secondary Slave Hard Disk Error	The IDE/ATAPI device configured as Secondary Slave could not be properly initialised by the BIOS. This message is typically displayed when the BIOS is trying to detect and configure IDE/ATAPI devices in POST.
Primary Master Drive – ATAPI Incompatible	The IDE/ATAPI device configured as Primary Master failed an ATAPI compatibility test. This message is typically displayed when the BIOS is trying to detect and configure IDE/ATAPI devices in POST.
Primary Slave Drive – ATAPI Incompatible	The IDE/ATAPI device configured as Primary Slave failed an ATAPI compatibility test. This message is typically displayed when the BIOS is trying to detect and configure IDE/ATAPI devices in POST.
Secondary Master Drive – ATAPI Incompatible	The IDE/ATAPI device configured as Secondary Master failed an ATAPI compatibility test. This message is typically displayed when the BIOS is trying to detect and configure IDE/ATAPI devices in POST.
Secondary Slave Drive – ATAPI Incompatible	The IDE/ATAPI device configured as Secondary Slave failed an ATAPI compatibility test. This message is typically displayed when the BIOS is trying to detect and configure IDE/ATAPI devices in POST.
S.M.A.R.T. Capable but Command Failed	The BIOS tried to send a S.M.A.R.T. message to a hard disk, but the command transaction failed. This message can be reported by an ATAPI device using the S.M.A.R.T. error reporting standard. S.M.A.R.T. failure messages may indicate the need to replace the hard disk.
S.M.A.R.T. Command Failed	The BIOS tried to send a S.M.A.R.T. message to a hard disk, but the command transaction failed. This message can be reported by an ATAPI device using the S.M.A.R.T. error reporting standard. S.M.A.R.T. failure messages may indicate the need to replace the hard disk.
S.M.A.R.T. Status BAD, Backup and Replace	A S.M.A.R.T. capable hard disk sends this message when it detects an imminent failure. This message can be reported by an ATAPI device using the S.M.A.R.T. error reporting standard. S.M.A.R.T. failure messages may indicate the need to replace the hard disk.
S.M.A.R.T. Capable and Status BAD	A S.M.A.R.T. capable hard disk sends this message when it detects an imminent failure. This message can be reported by an ATAPI device using the S.M.A.R.T. error reporting standard. S.M.A.R.T. failure messages may indicate the need to replace the hard disk.

AMI BIOS error codes continued:

Error	Action
BootSector Write!!	The BIOS has detected software attempting to write to a drive's boot sector. This is flagged as possible virus activity. This message will only be displayed if Virus Detection is enabled in AMIBIOS Setup.
VIRUS: Continue (Y/N)?	If the BIOS detects possible virus activity, it will prompt the user. This message will only be displayed if Virus Detection is enabled in AMIBIOS Setup.
DMA-2 Error	Error initialising secondary DMA controller. This is a fatal error, often indicating a problem with system hardware.
DMA Controller Error	POST error while trying to initialise the DMA controller. This is a fatal error, often indicating a problem with system hardware.
CMOS Date/Time Not Set	The CMOS Date and/or Time are invalid. This error can be resolved by readjusting the system time in AMIBIOS Setup.
CMOS Battery Low	CMOS Battery is low. This message usually indicates that the CMOS battery needs to be replaced. It could also appear when the user intentionally discharges the CMOS battery.
CMOS Settings Wrong	CMOS settings are invalid. This error can be resolved by using AMIBIOS Setup.
CMOS Checksum Bad	CMOS contents failed the Checksum check. Indicates that the CMOS data has been changed by a program other than the BIOS or that the CMOS is not retaining its data due to malfunction. This error can typically be resolved by using AMIBIOS Setup.
Keyboard Error	Keyboard is not present or the hardware is not responding when the keyboard controller is initialized.
Keyboard/Interface Error	Keyboard Controller failure. This may indicate a problem with system hardware.
System Halted	The system has been halted. A reset or power cycle is required to reboot the machine. This message appears after a fatal error has been detected.

Award BIOS beep codes

Number of Beeps	Problem	Action
1 long beep followed by 2 short beeps	Video card problem	Remove the card, clean the connecting edge that plugs into the motherboard socket, and replace. If that doesn't work, try an alternative video card to establish whether the problem lies with the card or the AGP slot. If you are using integrated video instead of a video card, the motherboard may be faulty.
Any other beeps	Memory problem	Remove each memory module, clean the connecting edge that plugs into the motherboard socket, and replace. If that doesn't work, try restarting with a single memory module and see if you can identify the culprit by a process of elimination. If you still get the error code, replace with known good modules.
1 long, 3 short	No detectable video card, or bad video card memory.	Ensure video card is correctly installed and powered. If it still occurs, there is a fault with the video card's memory.
High frequency beeps while running	Overheating CPU.	A sign that your CPU is not being cooled properly. First check the cooling systems are powered and functioning. If problems persist, first replace thermal paste and – if still occurring – install more efficient cooling systems.
Repeating high/low beeps	Fault with CPU.	Check that the CPU is seated properly in its socket. If it is, the CPU may be damaged. This may also occur if the CPU's heat is too much, follow above resolutions.

Award BIOS error codes Here are the standard Award onscreen error messages:

Error	Action
BIOS ROM checksum error – System halted	The checksum of the BIOS code in the BIOS chip is incorrect, indicating the BIOS code may have become corrupt. Contact your system dealer to replace the BIOS.
CMOS battery failed	The CMOS battery is no longer functional. Contact your system dealer for a replacement battery.
CMOS checksum error – Defaults loaded	Checksum of CMOS is incorrect, so the system loads the default equipment configuration. A checksum error may indicate that CMOS has become corrupt. This error may have been caused by a weak battery. Check the battery and replace if necessary.
CPU at nnnn	Displays the running speed of the CPU.
Display switch is set incorrectly	The display switch on the motherboard can be set to either monochrome or colour. This message indicates the switch is set to a different setting from that indicated in Setup. Determine which setting is correct, and then either turn off the system and change the jumper, or enter Setup and change the VIDEO selection.
Press ESC to skip memory test	The user may press Esc to skip the full memory test.
Floppy disk(s) fail	Cannot find or initialise the floppy drive controller or the drive. Make sure the controller is installed correctly. If no floppy drives are installed, be sure the Diskette Drive selection in Setup is set to NONE or AUTO.
HARD DISK initializing. Please wait a moment.	Some hard drives require extra time to initialise.
HARD DISK INSTALL FAILURE	Cannot find or initialise the hard drive controller or the drive. Make sure the controller is installed correctly. If no hard drives are installed, be sure the Hard Drive selection in Setup is set to NONE.
Hard disk(s) diagnosis fail	The system may run specific disk diagnostic routines. This message appears if one or more hard disks return an error when the diagnostics run.
Keyboard error or no keyboard present	Cannot initialise the keyboard. Make sure the keyboard is attached correctly and no keys are pressed during POST. To purposely configure the system without a keyboard, set the error halt condition in Setup to HALT ON ALL, BUT KEYBOARD. The BIOS then ignores the missing keyboard during POST.
Keyboard is locked out – Unlock the key	This message usually indicates that one or more keys have been pressed during the keyboard tests. Be sure no objects are resting on the keyboard.
Memory Test	This message displays during a full memory test, counting down the memory areas being tested.
Memory test fail	If POST detects an error during memory testing, additional information appears giving specifics about the type and location of the memory error.
Override enabled – Defaults loaded	If the system cannot boot using the current CMOS configuration, the BIOS can override the current configuration with a set of BIOS defaults designed for the most stable, minimal-performance system operations.
Press TAB to show POST screen	System OEMs may replace the Phoenix Technologies' AwardBIOS POST display with their own proprietary display. Including this message in the OEM display permits the operator to switch between the OEM display and the default POST display.
Primary master hard disk fail	POST detects an error in the primary master IDE hard drive.
Primary slave hard disk fail	POST detects an error in the primary slave IDE hard drive.
Secondary master hard disk fail	POST detects an error in the secondary master IDE hard drive.
Secondary slave hard disk fail	POST detects an error in the secondary slave IDE hard drive.

Index